Stepping Stones
A Therapeutic Adventure Activity Guide

ACTIVITIES TO ENHANCE OUTCOMES
WITH ALTERNATIVE POPULATIONS

EDITED BY

Peter Aubry

Project Adventure, Inc.
Advancing Active Learning

ISBN: 0-934387-31-6

Acknowledgments

This Activity Guide represents the work and contributions of many people affiliated with Project Adventure over the past three years. Its original inception was based on the work conducted at our Covington, Georgia Project Adventure Kids site. At this site, students, clinicians and staff in our Academic, Independent Living, Residential, Child and Adolescent Programs experienced, utilized, and created most of the activities you will find in this book. The core list of activities grew as a result of on-going work and training conducted with other Project Adventure clients. The results are these success-oriented activities that have demonstrated the ability to achieve desired social emotional outcomes with a variety of populations. It is hoped that this text will help you bring experiential learning activities and outcomes to life with your students in a productive, engaging and enjoyable manner. It has been a pleasure to work with all of the contributors and personnel who have participated in the creation of this Activity Guide.

Special thanks go to:

- Cindy Simpson and Mary Jane Worstell whose work in our Georgia program inspired the concept for this book. Mary Jane and her students were the primary drivers behind the initial phases of production.

- The students in our PA Kids programs who helped test, revise and create many of these activities. You are an inspiration to us all.

- Carol James whose on-going work with Project Adventure clients added proven activities and enhanced many of the activity write-ups. Her feedback proved invaluable! Carol along with Jean Walsh spent countless hours refining write-ups and making them as clear as possible so that readers would easily understand the framing, procedures and debriefings for each activity. Jean's patience in organizing and reorganizing the structure and flow of this guide is greatly appreciated.

- Karen Wright from Stillwater Residential Treatment Facility in New York and Dan Frances from Schimmell School of the Harrisburg School District in Pennsylvania whose reading and subsequent feedback on this text made it better and more practical. Their perspectives as Program Director and Psychologist respectively added tremendous value!

- MB Buckner, Bart Crawford, Rufus Collinson, Aaron Nicholson, Jane Panicucci, Dick Prouty, Paul Radcliffe and Jim Schoel whose review, feedback, dialogue and support added value all along the way.

- Ila Prouty whose critical eye and attention to detail drove a solid connection between social emotional learning outcomes and activity debriefs. Her organizational detail is greatly appreciated.

- Beth Wonson, without whose drive, dedication, determination and follow-through this project would not have been completed!

Contents

Introduction to Adventure

WHAT IS ADVENTURE PROGRAMMING?

Adventure is a *way* of doing; it is not just an activity in and of itself. If the word adventure conjures up images of wilderness camping, rock climbing, rafting and parachuting, pause for a moment and imagine instead the *way* in which an activity is performed. A group session or class becomes an adventure for students if there is an element of surprise and if the class is intentionally designed so that the collaborative activities compel them to interact in pro-social ways they have never before experienced. Adventure exists when participants become engaged, not because they are mandated to participate or earn points, but because they are having meaningful and relevant experiences that build belief in their own abilities. Adventure includes challenge – moments when students are on the brink of both success and failure and where they both succeed and fail. The challenge occurs in an emotionally and physically safe environment where frustration and healthy conflict can be managed when both success and failure are imminent. Within that environment, students are supported to try new approaches, strategies and tools for coping and managing their emotions and interactions. Adventure is about taking risks – emotional and apparent risks where participants consider and learn decision-making within the natural and logical consequences before them. For students to participate in a program like this, an atmosphere of safety needs to exist, a space where students can speak their minds and push themselves to limits.

For vulnerable, at-risk and mentally challenged children and youth to participate in any program that includes challenge, risk and intentionally tapping into the remediation of reactions to stressors and triggers, there needs to be, along with an atmosphere of safety, skilled staff who can manage and maintain an environment in which participants can speak their minds and push their limits. Staff need to guide students as they struggle to learn to manage their own emotions, reactions, decisions and consequences while learning what it means to be a positive, supportive and empathetic member of a group. Additionally, there need to be moments of celebration, laughter and fun! Yes, all of this can happen in a class, a therapeutic recreation program, alternative school, residential treatment or a lock up….with no parachute ever opened, no cliff ever scaled and no wilderness camping! This is adventure teaching and learning.

The activities in this book are intentionally designed for a wide variety of environments in which many teachers, clinicians and therapists work with children and youth of various populations. The activities have been developed by and for professionals like you. The methodology, adventure teaching and learning presented in this book, has been used extensively in schools, treatment centers, juvenile justice programs and hospitals since 1980.

An activity in and of itself is just that – a recreational environment. With vulnerable and at-risk children and youth, activities can evoke reactions that need to be appropriately responded to and resolved. These activities, when used along with the foundational concepts of Project Adventure methodology, become therapeutic tools and part of the healing, recovery and skill development process. These foundational concepts will be introduced at the beginning of this text. This text should not be considered a substitute for appropriate training in adventure programming or a particular professional discipline. It is intended to supplement what already exists in your current program or class. Adventure adds new activities, and a new methodology, to the teaching, therapy and counseling. We believe that you and your students will find these activities and this methodology to be exhilarating and powerful.

WHY USE ADVENTURE PROGRAMMING

The vast majority of adventure activities require students to develop problem-solving skills and experience success in solving problems. Adolescents who are able to solve problems are more resilient and less likely to suffer negative psychological consequences than those who avoid problems.[1]

In adventure activities, students are asked to focus on their abilities rather than their inabilities. This orientation can diminish initial defenses to change and actually lead to healthy change. Students experience success and mastery as they complete progressively difficult and rewarding tasks. You will frame your student's efforts to center on the potential to increase their character strengths such as emotional stability, decision making, assertiveness, and social competence. In short, a well-run therapeutic adventure program empowers students to develop lifelong social skills and strong character traits.

The following are more reasons why adventure is such a powerful tool for helping students to manage their own behavior:

- Adventure, when well presented, is engaging – it is fun and students want to participate.
- Adventure learning allows students to experience a behavior (positive or not), reflect on that behavior, learn to replicate or diminish (as is appropriate) that behavior and learn to transfer that behavior to other settings.
- Adventure requires students to be responsible to self, community and others.
- Adventure requires students to grow.
- Adventure allows the teacher/facilitator/counselor to observe students using social emotional skills – enabling them to more accurately assess student progress.

---

1. Dumont, M. & Provost M. (1999) "Resilience in Adolescents: Protective Role of Social Support, Coping Strategies, Self-Esteem, and Social Activities on Experience of Stress and Depression." *Journal of Youth and Adolescence* 28.3.: Ebata, A. T., and Moos, R. H. (1995). "Personal, situational, and contextual correlates of coping in adolescence." J. Res. Adolesc. 4: 99-125. & Herman-Stahl, M. A., Stemmler, M., and Petersen, A. C. (1995). "Approach and avoidant coping: Implications for adolescent mental health." *Journal of Youth and Adolescence.* 24.

WHAT IS PROJECT ADVENTURE?

Project Adventure is an international nonprofit organization with a simple goal: "To bring the adventure home" to children, youth and adults. Our roots, incorporating counseling and adventure, are more than 30 years deep, with our first program implementation in 1971. PA's founders, former Outward Bound instructors, had experience in leading wilderness adventure trips. Struck by the power of adventure, but understanding that it is more about doing and less about where and what one does, they developed a program that could be done in facilities or on an athletic or playground field. The goal was to make adventure accessible to people of all abilities and adaptable to many different time frames. From the moment when adventure was first implemented in a public school counseling environment more than 30 years ago, the program has been engaging the disengaged, developing respectful communities in schools and agencies and supporting participants to build skills to stay in or return to the least restrictive environment.

Adventure Based Counseling continues to be one of the models at the core of Project Adventure's work. Thousands of counselors, educators and recreational therapists have implemented the foundational concepts of Adventure Based Counseling (ABC) in their programs throughout the US, and internationally. Project Adventure also conducts a continuum of direct service programs in Covington, GA and with school districts and agencies who have become licensees, using ABC [Behavior Management Through Adventure] holistically throughout their whole milieu. Our original ABC text, *Islands of Healing* by Schoel, Prouty and Radcliffe has been published both in English and Japanese and continues to be considered a "must read" in the world of Adventure Therapy / Counseling along with its complement *Exploring Islands of Healing* by Schoel and Maizell.

Foundational Concepts

Full Value Contract

The Full Value Contract (FVC) is a cornerstone of a well-run adventure program and critical to the effective use of the activities in this guide. The FVC is responsible for creating an environment where students feel safe enough to take risks. The FVC also serves as a structure for creating behavioral norms that everyone agrees to follow and maintain throughout the life of the activity, class, session; and in the case of a full-school or agency implementation, all the time and in all interactions. This norm-setting process establishes an atmosphere of caring, feeling connected and of feeling valued. This atmosphere is critical to students' being able to participate fully in adventure activities.

There are a number of ways to develop Full Value Contracts. The Full Value Contract chapter of this book will take you through developing and creating a Full Value Contract with many enhancing adventure activities. As group members participate in and become more familiar with the use of the FVC, the norms will actually promote pro-social behavior and actively prevent explosive and destructive behaviors. Used effectively, the FVC becomes the common language and guide for daily interactions between student and student and students and staff. Not only will you as a facilitator be able to help students explore, understand and value healthy, pro-social behaviors, but you will also be able to help students transfer the use of the FVC to the next placement or other environments like their home.

Challenge by Choice®

Thirty years of counseling and teaching using adventure has taught us many lessons. One of the most powerful lessons involves the use of choice. Coaxing or mandating students to participate only teaches them (or in the case of the children and youth you serve – reinforces for them) that they can be talked into doing something. On the other hand, helping students to see that they have the ability and right to choose their level of participation, and how to access what is and isn't an appropriate level of challenge, teaches them how to make positive decisions for life. Progressively empowering students to positively exercise choice by integrating Challenge by Choice into your work is critical to the well-run adventure program.

Challenge by Choice does not assume that you will continually allow students to opt out of activities because that is what they chose. A way to understand the concept of Challenge by Choice is by looking at the optimal learning zone. Most of us can recognize three different zones within which we function: comfort, stretch and panic. (See graphic).

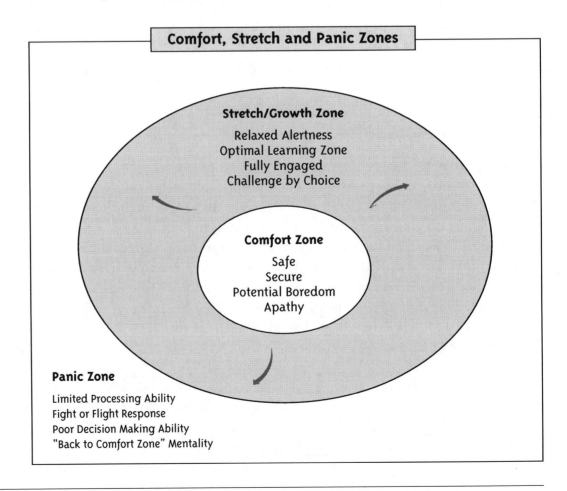

Comfort, Stretch and Panic Zones

Stretch/Growth Zone
Relaxed Alertness
Optimal Learning Zone
Fully Engaged
Challenge by Choice

Comfort Zone
Safe
Secure
Potential Boredom
Apathy

Panic Zone
Limited Processing Ability
Fight or Flight Response
Poor Decision Making Ability
"Back to Comfort Zone" Mentality

Challenge by Choice strives to have students learn how to participate in their stretch zones while learning to avoid or not choose situations that put them in their panic zones. The core element here is that students look to determine how they can add value to an activity while challenging themselves.

You will be able to recognize which zone your students are in during activities (and at other times). When students are in their comfort zones, they are often bored, not challenged and disengaged. Students in their panic zones are frequently hyper-vigilant, anxious and will do anything to remove themselves from the anxiety-provoking situation. A student in the panic zone has a very difficult time learning and processing new information. Therefore it is critical to help students determine what their stretch zone looks like. The next step is to assist them in identifying goals, tools and strategies to challenge themselves by working in and experiencing their stretch zones more deeply. From this will come learning, discovery and feedback that will help them to grow.

As a facilitator, you will have much more success if you keep the concept of Challenge by Choice in mind as you conduct the activities in this book. Remember that while not participating is not an option, it is also true that not everyone has to participate in the same way and at the same level to challenge themselves. Students who appear to be in their comfort zone should be challenged into their stretch zone. Conversely, students who appear to be in their panic zone should be supported in finding a way to participate in their stretch zone. Work with your students using this model to help identify ways they can work with each other so that they might engage more in their stretch or challenge zones.

Experiential Learning and the Experiential Learning Cycle

This activity guide is experiential and based on the theory of experiential learning. The Experiential Learning Cycle (shown in the following graphic) explains the rationale for the activity structure used in this activity guide.

The Experiential Learning Cycle was developed from David Kolb's learning theory model (Kolb, D. A. (1984) Experiential Learning, Englewood Cliffs, NJ.: Prentice Hall). It tells us that helping students to experience a seemingly isolated event (the activity) and giving it context (helping them to create meaning from it) provides them with the opportunity to learn, understand, apply and transfer knowledge.

Kolb highlights the four phases of a learning cycle: concrete experience, reflective observation, abstract conceptualization and active experimentation.

Once an activity has been completed, a period of reflecting (or debriefing) helps students to draw relevance from the experience. Connecting the present experience to past experiences also enhances learning. During this phase, the simple questions, "What happened in the activity?", "So, what can we learn from what occurred?" or "Now what can we do with this information?" provide the structure (see graphic). Activities without this structure limit potential learning opportunities for our students.

The Experiential Learning Cycle

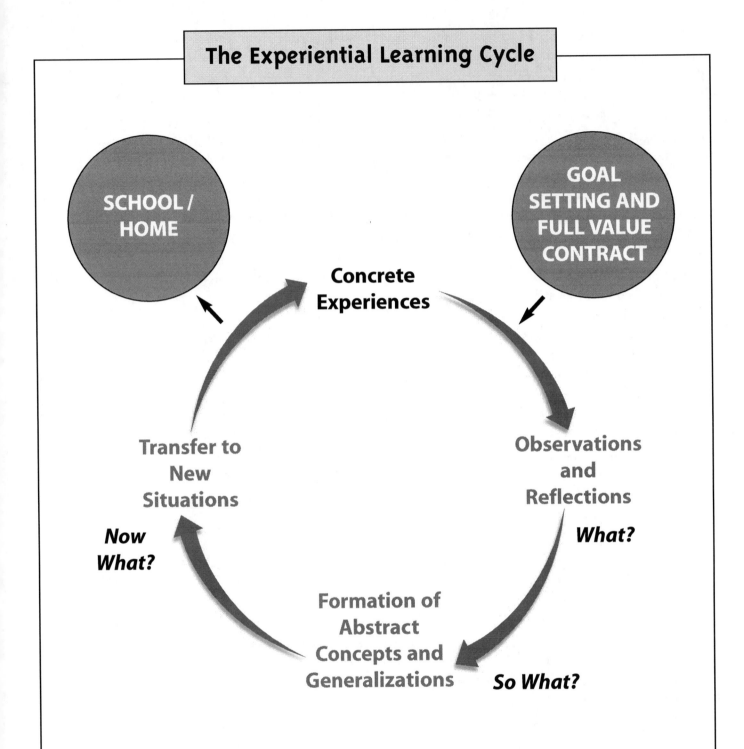

I see, and I forget.
    I hear, and I remember.
        I do, and I understand.

—ancient Chinese proverb

The Adventure Integrated Model developed by Project Adventure, enhances the ELC by:

- Highlighting the importance of aligning activities with goals (Goal Setting)
- Identifying the need to promote group development – norms and the ability to care for one another as vital to effective experiential learning (Full Value Contract)
- Expanding the reflected process (reflection) to broader life experiences – the Now What? Discussion includes how behavior and attitude affects the student group in your program and "real life."
- Empowering students to be active and participatory learners by asking them to define their own challenges – for optimal learning (Challenge by Choice).

Goal Setting

The process of goal setting is a key element in an adventure program. It is also key to fostering resiliency among vulnerable and at-risk youth. Research has consistently shown that having a sense of purpose, which includes being able to set and attain goals, is a significant way that resiliency is manifested. Helping students to set and attain goals is one of the fundamental skills for success that is taught through the activities in this guide. Goal setting requires the ability to see what needs to be accomplished to attain a goal, plan a series of steps and follow those steps to goal attainment. Making positive choices and then pursuing them is the action of goal setting. Adventure activities provide safe opportunities for practicing and reflecting on goal setting and attainment. Through the adventure group process, facilitators and peers are also modeling goal setting and attainment.

Students need to set their own goals within the context of the goals of the program and the Full Value Contract. To help students be as successful as possible with goal work, Project Adventure utilizes SMART Goals as a tool.

S-Specific	Set one goal at a time – with no alternatives or "outs." If the goal is changed, that must be negotiated and the goal must be restated. Goals can be added but not at the expense of the original goal.
M-Measurable	Frequency and/or quantity (how much or how often) are examples of measurements.
A-Achievable	There must be a chance of success. Setting impossible goals allows us to avoid responsibility. Setting goals that are achievable with some challenge increases confidence, competency and efficacy.
R-Relevant	Is it important to pursue this goal? Is it a goal that has already been achieved and therefore not a challenge? Can other goals be built upon this one? Does achieving this goal support you toward attaining a bigger goal?
T-Trackable	Can you tell if you have completed part or all of the goal at a specific time?

Additional Concepts to Consider

Creating a learning Community

Adventure theory and learning theory tell us that in order to effectively learn, we must feel safe – emotionally and physically. Geoffrey and Renate Caine, learning theorists who have integrated neuroscience, biological and psychological research to help us understand how people learn, explain that human beings cannot learn when they are afraid:

> "For every human being on the planet, from birth 'til death, threat tied to fear and helplessness sabotages the most promising kind of learning, including higher order thinking (executive functions). Relaxed alertness is the ideal mental state for higher order functioning. Creating an environment that fosters this mental state must be a primary goal for teachers, therapists, and educators."[2]

They describe relaxed alertness as "consisting of low threat and high challenge" delivered most effectively in an environment that supports social and emotional development.[3] What are the tools for helping your students attain relaxed alertness – how do you operationalize this? Adventure education provides us with some essential structures.

As adventure facilitators, the language we use and the behaviors we reinforce send a powerful message. As we offer activities and hold students to behavioral norms, we must consciously use language that helps students build on their assets. Doing so will demonstrate your commitment to these important and effective concepts. Granted, this is more work than telling your students what to do, but the results are well worth it. They will actively take responsibility for their learning and support their peers in doing the same.

Some asset-focused words and phrases are:

- Try that again. Let's see how it goes this time.

- You can do it.

- I am here, but you don't need me to figure this out.

- How do you think we should handle it when…? (Not telling students what to do or not do, but inviting them to be part of the solution.)

- I appreciated it when… (Acknowledging and celebrating positive behavior)

- What did it feel like when…? (Acknowledging and respecting feelings)

Adventure learning is holistic in that it addresses students in their entirety – as thinking, feeling, physical and emotional beings. It permits young people to practice making choices they might not ordinarily make as well as observe peers practicing behaviors that might not ordinarily seem possible. "If we create a class-

2. http://www.cainelearning.com/principle11.html
3. Caine & Caine; Making Connections: Learning and the Human Brain; 1994; Addison-Wesley

room community, we can then learn what it means to be members of that community. If we want students to act responsibly, we must give them responsibility. This microcosm of 'the real world' is at the core of experiential education: to learn by doing, and to gain insight from the experience."[4]

Social Emotional Learning and Adventure Learning

Social emotional learning (SEL) is necessary for children to develop into competent caring people who make good decisions and have positive relationships. *"To best develop these capacities, children need to experience safe, nurturing, and well-managed environments where they feel valued and respected; they need meaningful interactions with socially and emotionally competent others; and they need positive and specific guidance. Thus, SEL takes place within the context of safe school, family, and community environments that support children's development and provide opportunities and recognition for successfully applying these competencies."*[5]

Adventure activities do that by (1) focusing on community creation, (2) asking students to be responsible to self and others and (3) having specific SEL skills significantly positioned among its learning themes. Some specific, but not all SEL learning themes that the activities in the guide focus on are:

- Identify and manage one's emotions and behavior.
- Recognize personal qualities and external supports
- Demonstrate skills related to achieving personal goals.
- Recognize the feelings and perspectives of others.
- Recognize individual and group similarities and differences.
- Use communication and social skills to interact effectively with others.
- Demonstrate an ability to prevent, manage, and resolve interpersonal conflicts in constructive ways.
- Consider ethical, safety, and societal factors in making decisions.
- Apply decision-making skills to deal responsibly with daily academic and social situations.
- Contribute to the well-being of one's school and community.

Importantly, students in Project Adventure programs experience safe, nurturing, and well-managed environments where they feel valued and respected and they have meaningful interactions with socially and emotionally competent others. So not only do Project Adventure activities intentionally promote specific social emotional skills, but they create a safe environment in which students can grow and develop.

4. Frank, Laurie; The Caring Classroom; Project Adventure, Inc; 2001
5. http://www.casel.org/basics/definition.php

About This Activity Guide

This activity guide is intended to be a resource for anyone implementing adventure with at-risk, alternative school or therapeutic populations. The activities are intentionally designed to support programs that seek to: remediate or increase social skills, improve behaviors, heal and support recovery from mental health issues including trauma or to support students who have been unsuccessful in traditional educational settings.

The desired results of this activity guide are to provide opportunities for participants to:

1. Understand and contribute to the development of Full Value Contract.
2. Manage and assess behaviors in alignment with the Full Value Contract.
3. Demonstrate an ability to set and achieve appropriate group and individual goals.
4. Demonstrate the ability to form positive relationships.
5. Develop appropriate responses to one's own, and others' emotions.
6. Demonstrate the ability to be accountable and to make appropriate and responsible decisions.
7. Develop and/or enhance empathy for others.

> **Please Note:**
> Although this guide can be used for juvenile halls, court schools, alternative schools, residential treatment programs, youth ranches, etc. — for the sake of uniformity and clarity, we will refer to the participants — the children and youth — as students. The word *students* in this guide refers to residents, wards, patients, clients and students.

How to use this activity guide

The book is organized into four chapters with an introduction to the use of adventure as a learning methodology. Each chapter has a brief introduction explaining the relevance of and practical issues for the chapter's theme. A chapter contains sections that focus on various learning themes that are tied directly to the aforementioned desired results. Each section also provides an introduction further explaining the section's theme and intent.

From our experience, the activities in each section are very effective in achieving the desired results. Given that this is a Guide and not a Curriculum, the activities are not sequential. We have organized the activities in alphabetical order in each Section of this Guide (except the Full Value section) based on the name of the activity. You should assess what your group needs, determine which of the four chapters and their sections you should review, then select the activity and learning theme that ties directly to the goals of your program or class. As you familiarize yourself with these activities, you should be able to utilize your experience and professional skills to modify them to fit the specific needs of the population you are serving.

Project Adventure's foundational concepts within this Introductory Chapter will provide you with a framework for conducting the activities. These adventure activities are the vehicle through which your students will practice, experience and learn skills and behaviors that will lead them to becoming empathetic, responsible, capable and competent individual and team members. The activities are intended to provide you with structure, not dictate your curriculum and can either stand alone or be implemented in conjunction with other curricula you are delivering. Again, take what you need.

Our recommendation is that you begin by reading the Introduction and become familiar with the theory upon which adventure teaching and learning is based. Preview what you can expect your students to learn through the effective application of the core elements and activities. Many facilitators, counselors and educators also participate in a Project Adventure training to complement what they learn through our texts. Our immersion approach to training allows an opportunity for you to experience the activities and the adventure process in the same way your students will. This experience not only provides great insight but greatly enhances your ability and outcomes.

How to use the activity descriptions

Activities (except for the Full Value activities) are listed alphabetically within their given section. Each activity has a title and information on how to conduct that activity and the materials you will need to run it. Each activity provides learning themes that are aligned with the desired results explained earlier in this chapter.

Each activity has a brief description that includes:

- Description – a quick overview of the activity

- Learning Themes – subjects chosen to provide learning opportunities for students

- Estimated Time – an approximate time frame (it is important to note that the length of time for each activity will vary greatly depending upon your group's need for processing behaviors and/or feelings that arise during a given activity)

- Props – what you'll need to facilitate each activity

- Setup – how and what you'll need to prepare to facilitate each activity

- Framing – a script to help your students think about the relevance of the experience they are about to have (the script can be used verbatim, but is offered mainly as a guideline)

- Procedure – the rules and guidelines for each activity

- Reflection – questions for discussion and/or activities for reflection that will help your students look at the "What?" "Now what?" and "So what?" of the Experiential Learning Cycle

Additionally, you will find boxes with facilitation tips, variations of many of the activities as well as additional thoughts and safety checks as appropriate.

Unless otherwise mentioned, framing and reflection should happen with the group standing or sitting in a circle. You may want to participate in or observe the reflection process. Do whatever is appropriate to your goals for the group at the time.

Please note:

1. Although we have categorized activities, the themes and sections are designed primarily to provide guidance. There is a lot of overlap in themes or potential themes for activities. So, feel free to mix and swap the activities.

2. We have explained this in numerous places throughout the text, but it can't be overstated. If there is something that happens during an activity that you need to resolve or explore during the reflection, do so. Don't feel limited to the reflection we've designed.

Important Assumptions

TRAINING: The outcomes of these activities are greatly enhanced through appropriate training. A "well-run adventure program" typically includes staff who are trained in the use of adventure and always includes Project Adventure's foundational concepts, introduced in this Chapter. Project Adventure suggests a comprehensive training plan that addresses the following key areas:

- Basic theory of adventure and experiential education
- Experiencing of activities including warm-ups, ice-breakers and initiatives
- Facilitation, processing and debriefing skills
- Techniques for goal setting and group development
- Safety and risk management skills appropriate for the activities in this book

PROPS AND EQUIPMENT: Each activity includes a list of props that are necessary. Many props are available in your existing equipment rooms or storage closets. Project Adventure offers a Portable Adventure Challenge Kit (Pack Bag) designed specifically to accompany this activity guide as well as individual items for purchase.

The activities in this guide do not use any high or low challenge course elements. Low challenge course elements are an excellent tool for group problem solving, conflict resolution and processing. High challenge course elements are used extensively as peak experiences and build trust, competency, help students break through perceived limitations and are exhilarating. Project Adventure is the pioneer in designing, installing, maintaining and providing training in the use of challenge courses. As you develop your adventure program, consider adding these elements to further enhance the value this program affords your students.

ASSESSMENT: Assessment is a critical component of any program. It is important to not only assess individual and group goal achievement but also overall program goals. Individual and group assessment frequency varies depending on the population you are working with; however, we advocate that daily check-ins be done on personal goals or at the minimum, weekly. In Chapter 2: Learning to Assess My Group and Self, you will find activities that will assist you and your students in evaluating their personal and group goals and performance. However you will not find activities or tools to assess your overall program goals.

acquire through participation in this program.

Chapter One:
Full Value Community

The **Full Value Contract (FVC)** is a powerful tool for creating behavioral norms and values (See Introduction.) It is fundamental to a good adventure program because it enables you and your students to create community.

The FVC is composed of six components:

- **Be Here** – be fully present – i.e., cell phones are turned off, MP3s are put away, attendance is important, paying attention is important, etc.
- **Be Safe** – physically and emotionally – i.e., it is important to tell others what you need, feedback is given in a way that respects the recipients (no yelling or intimidating), activities are well spotted, etc.
- **Be Honest** – giving and receiving feedback – some ways this is translated into behavior are: speaking your truth, accepting responsibility for your behavior (good and bad), etc.
- **Set Goals** – attainable and positive – the students set goals, students support others' goals, students know others' goals, etc.
- **Care for Self and Others** – being a responsible member of the community – students check in with each other regarding how they are feeling; students hold themselves and each other responsible to the norms established in their Full Value Contract, etc.
- **Let Go and Move On** – using feedback for growth – students discuss and resolve issues as they arise. A resolved issue is not discussed again. Students' behaviors reflect the understanding that disagreements do not make enemies, etc.

These components are used to form a framework under which your norms and your students' norms will fit. The components guide the activity selection and learning themes for this section.

The norms need to be ones that both staff and students agree to, will use and will be responsible to. As staff, you should be part of the group when developing *your* Full Value Contract and in sharing the norms and values that are important to you. However, let the group take the lead. Your role is to ask clarifying questions and to add any non-negotiable norms that they haven't already added – like no violence or no drugs.

Developing a Full Value Contract cannot be a voting activity – the group must achieve agreement on each behavioral norm. Otherwise, it won't work. Determine a method to symbolize consensus around and commitment to the agreed-upon norms. Some group leaders will have their students sign the Contract and others prefer to make it a verbal or thumbs up/down agreement. Keep in mind that signing can be more of a commitment than a verbal or thumbs up/down agreement.

The norms and values created in the Full Value Contract are target behaviors for which the group will strive. None of us are perfect; therefore students are striving to meet the norms and in this process learning occurs through the use of Full

Value. There will be times when students do not follow the norms or "mess up." Once norms and values have been agreed upon, systems to reinforce them need to be developed. The group and its leader (you) need to develop these systems for reinforcing the norms and values with your group. The following is an example of how this discussion might be led.

> "If someone is off a behavioral target (operating outside the Full Value Contract norms) not honoring our commitment, e.g., blurting out "That's a stupid idea!", what should we do to remind her of her commitment? Can we come up with a word (sign, activity, etc) to remind her without yelling or devaluing her?"

In BMTA programs, this is typically a time when staff and/or students "call group." Group is called when something specific and serious and 'issue-oriented' has happened and must be dealt with immediately. A key ingredient in the empowerment of students is represented in the learning of the "call group" skill.

The FVC is most successful when members of the community (staff and students) begin to develop relationships through intentionally-designed adventure activities. The community must have an understanding of the expectations and goals of the program before beginning the Full Value Contract. Otherwise, groups will just write down what they think you want to hear – respect, teamwork, honesty – without really thinking about what they are saying.

Facilitators have found that most groups are ready for norm setting after about four hours of working together. Four hours of working together means interacting, playing, problem-solving, etc. as a team. For example, your students will not be ready for norm setting after four hours of watching a video, doing homework, etc. Activities for building a FVC are contained in this chapter.

Reflect on your FVC daily or regularly (depending on how often you meet). The Full Value Contract is an important program element that should be added to and subtracted from as appropriate. It will develop with your group. It is not a tool for strictly enforcing the rules, to help you control your students: "You didn't let each other speak and your Full Value Contract says you will." Rather, as stated above, it is a tool that will help the group develop social and emotional skills. Strive to empower your students to assess their own progress, e.g., "How do you think you're doing with listening to and not talking over each other? Is there anything that we could improve upon? What are we doing really well?"

Evaluating your FVC and how well the group is meeting the norms and values could be your ritual for beginning a program day. Tools to help you assess progress toward implementing the FVC are contained throughout this guide.

Ownership and empowerment are further enhanced by having students co-create symbols and posters and language of the FVC and displaying them prominently for all to see. Your FVC should grow and develop with your group. In order for it to provide you with the structure for norm creation, maintenance and development that you need, everyone needs to understand what it is. By hanging the posters prominently, you give your students a visual representation of the importance of the FVC in your school/program/agency.

This chapter will guide you through developing and creating a Full Value Contract along with adventure activities that explore the values in greater depth.

Section I: Creating Community/Full Value

This section introduces students to the Full Value Contract and helps them to understand and appreciate each value as an individual concept. They will become familiar with the six core values of the contract before understanding the Full Value Contract as a whole and developing their own FVC.

Through the activities in this section, students will be able to:

- Identify the six core values of the Full Value Contract.

- Recognize the importance of the six Full Values by describing how using these values will improve their lives and their participation in groups.

- Identify behaviors that reflect Full Value in self and others.

- Identify behaviors that conflict with Full Value in self and others.

- Begin to demonstrate behaviors consistent with the six Full Values.

Activities

The activities in this section are intended to be introduced sequentially, building upon each other in the traditional order of the Full Value Contract:

Be Here
Be Safe
Be Honest
Set Goals
Care for Self and Others
Let Go and Move On

Depending on the goals and your group, you may choose to alter the sequence or select only the activities that meet specific needs.

Activities:

- Full Value ESP
- Peek-A-Who
- Copy Cat
- Pigs in a Blanket
- Secret Agent
- Pairs Tag
- Out of Kilter
- Human Camera
- Stepping Stones
- Moon Ball
- Welded Ankles
- Dead Ant Tag
- 7, 11, 21
- Bear, Salmon, Mosquito

Full Value ESP

Description:

Full Value ESP is a fun movement activity that introduces students to the six components/core values of the Full Value Contract.

Learning Themes:

- Describe and demonstrate what it means to be a contributing member of a Full Value community.
- Understand and describe how the Full Value Contract can be an asset to their community.

Props:

None

Estimated Time

40 minutes

Tip:

For every activity in this guide, it is fine to return to it the next time you meet. For example, this activity could be done in two 20 minute segments. When appropriate or relevant, you may choose to stop and reflect on behaviors and feelings that arise.

Setup:

None

Framing:

"Today we are going to begin to learn about the Full Value Contract. The Full Value Contract is an agreement that we are going to work on together that will help us to learn to treat one another as we ourselves want to be treated. We are going to build a strong community together."

Procedure:

Preparation for the Activity:

1. Have students stand in a circle. Ask them to show you what it looks like when someone is "being here" in the classroom. You may need to spend some time discussing what "being here" means. For example: "Are you being here when you yawn? Are you being here when you join the discussion? Are you being here when you make eye contact with the person speaking?"

2. Mirror a few of the responses and then have the group pick an expressive gesture to represent being here through voting.

3. Together, the whole group should practice that gesture.

4. Repeat steps 1, 2 & 3 for "being safe."

5. Have the group repeat both gestures.

6. Repeat discussing, selecting and practicing a gesture for each of the six full values. The Full Values are: Be Here; Be Safe; Be Honest; Set Goals; Care for Self and Others and Let Go and Move On.

Tip:

If you have time, spend it reaching consensus on which gesture to pick and why the students thought it was the best representation of each value.

7. Have the group practice all six gestures.

8. Divide the group into pairs.

The Activity:

1. Explain to the group that they are going to have the opportunity to practice communicating with one another without talking.

2. Have the pairs turn back to back.

3. Explain that on the count of three, each member of the pairs will turn around and show one of the six gestures the group chose to represent a Full Value.

4. Explain that the goal is for them to communicate with each other without talking or signaling and show the same gesture.

5. For the first couple of rounds, you should count to three and ask the students to face each other with their gesture.

6. You can have them switch partners after three or so rounds. Stop while they are still engaged.

Reflection:

1. What was it like to try to connect with your partner without being able to talk or signal one another (verbal or non-verbal communication)?

2. Did your team have a strategy for trying to show the same gesture? If so, what was it?

3. What do you think of the Full Values?

4. How do you think the Full Values can help us work together?

5. How could you see using these values in our class/school/program/etc? Would anything be different if we did?

Peek-A-Who

Description:
Peek-A-Who is a fun and engaging activity that demonstrates the importance of knowing names of peers and generates good feelings about " Being Here."

Learning Themes:
- Know and appreciate one's peers.
- Demonstrate an understanding of each of the core Full Values.

Props:
- A tarp or sheet

Estimated Time
25 minutes

Setup:
Ask two students to hold the tarp or sheet between them. It should create a vertical barrier that can be raised and lowered easily. Divide the rest of the class into two groups, one on each side of the screen. Each group should sit on the ground.

Framing:
"Sometimes we can 'Be Here' just by knowing and learning how to connect with those around us."

Procedure:
ROUND 1: Ask one volunteer from each team to sit directly in front of their side of the screen. They need to do this quietly. When the screen is dropped, the two players must verbally identify each other by name. Whoever is the first to identify the other person correctly wins. The slower player moves over to the faster person's team. Only permit the two volunteers to speak; the rest of the players must remain silent. Play this several times.

ROUND 2: Ask groups of two, three or even four people to sit in front of the screen at the same time. This can vary each round. It is always the team that says the other teams' names first that gets to bring people to their side.
When there is only one large team, start again with a new twist.

ROUND 3: When the screen comes down, have the volunteers sit with their backs to one another. Their team then gives them hints about who the opposing player is. Hints can only describe positive qualities of the opposing player. (Physical and non physical, i.e., "Good basket ball player" "Naturally curly hair")
Whoever first identifies the other person correctly wins. The slower player moves over to the faster person's team.
When there is only one large team, the game is done!

ROUND 4: Use only things that you know about each other (not physical characteristics), (i.e., "Plays the piano," "Good at math").

Reflection:

1. How did it feel to change teams? Were you still rooting for your old team or were you immediately rooting for your new team?
2. How did it feel to have people know your name right away?
3. How did it feel to have your classmates say good things about you?
4. Was anyone surprised by what people said?
5. How does it help us to "Be Here" when we know and feel good about one another?

Copy Cat

Estimated Time

10 minutes

Tip:

This activity can go quickly, so feel free to play it two or three times.

Description:

Copy Cat is a quiet activity that enables students to practice Being Here.

Learning Themes:

- Understand what it is to focus on/pay attention to another.
- Analyze potential consequences of following others.

Props:

None

Setup:

Have students stand in a circle one arm-length apart.

Framing:

"Sometimes we can 'Be Here' by being really focused. Let's pay attention in this activity and see what we notice about each other."

Procedure:

The entire activity is played while standing in a large circle without changing positions.

1. Ask each student to, silently, without letting anyone in the group know, pick his or her leader from someone in the circle. No one is to reveal who his or her leader is.

2. Explain that in a moment everyone will be asked to shut their eyes and get into a unique pose. This pose must be done from where they are standing. Examples of poses include hands on hips, or legs crossed.

3. "When I ask you to open your eyes, you are to look at your leaders and change into your leader's pose. This should be done slowly and subtly, attempting to hide the identity of your leader."

4. "If your leader continues to change poses, keep changing your pose to match that of your leader, and remember do it so no one figures out who your leader is!"

5. End the activity when the majority of students have the same pose. Then ask students to point out their leaders.

6. Go right into a new round, before you stop to reflect, and ask students to pick different leaders and poses.

 Tip:

• *This might also be a place to talk about following someone.*

• *Capitalize on teachable moments.*

• *Use what happens in the activity as topics for reflection.*

• *Strengthen your counseling by giving students concrete evidence of what happened and reflect on what it means.*

Reflection:

1. What did you notice about how this activity ended?

2. Did anyone figure out who anyone else's leader was?

3. What were the clues you observed to figure this out?

4. Was there anyone so focused on his or her leader that they didn't notice what the rest of the group was doing?

5. How does what happened in this activity relate to our value of "Be Here?"

6. What are some of the ways that we just experienced Being Here that we can use in our classroom?

Pigs in a Blanket

Estimated Time

25 minutes

Description:

In this moderately active activity, students explore the "Be Safe" value.

Learning Themes:

- Describe the skills needed to set healthy personal and/or group goals.
- Learn to work together to achieve a common goal or task.

Props:

- 1 tarp per every 8-10 students
- Multiple tossables per every 8-10 students

Setup:

Ask your students to get into groups of eight to ten. Give each group a tarp to circle and to hold waist high.

Framing:

"Today we have some very special creatures to take care of." (Hold up a rubber chicken or pig or whatever tossable you have handy.) "We are going to be giving them a really fun ride, but we need to let them know how much fun they will have and how long we think the ride will last."

Procedure:

1. Let your students know that, using the tarps only they will be throwing and catching their critters. Everyone must keep one hand on the tarp at all times.

2. Start each group with their own rubber pig or chicken. Have groups practice throwing and catching their critters, using the tarp.

3. First, ask your students to practice how high they can toss their critters. Remind them the high toss only counts if they catch the critters after the toss! Then, have each group demonstrate their highest toss.

4. Have each group practice and demonstrate the highest number of consecutive tosses they can make. This means the number of tosses in a row without dropping the critters.

5. Give each group another tossable of a different size and weight; have them repeat the above steps with that object.

6. Given their results, ask the class to select the tossable that they would like to use for the next series of tasks. This time ask them to set a goal for how high (make sure you have a way of judging, e.g., over the blackboard or as high as that branch). Then, they should set a goal for how many times in a row, without dropping, they can throw their tossables.

7. Finally, challenge each group to throw (tarps only!) their tossable to another group, as well as to receive a tossable from that other group. You can keep score of how many successful throws and catches each group makes if that seems appropriate.

8. Do other variations (described below) if the group is still engaged.

Reflection:

Reflection Activity:

1. Have each group write a letter to their main critter (whatever they think that was) describing:
   - What skills they used to toss them high
   - What skills they used to toss them in a row
   - How they worked together to set goals
   - How they worked with the other team to send and receive critters

2. Encourage them to have fun writing the letter in a language the critter would understand (e.g., "We really oink, oink, had fun tossing you up to the oink, oink light and hearing you squeal.")

3. When they are ready or the time you've given them is up, have them read their letters.

Variations

- *Have your students set goals for throwing the tossables back and forth with the other team.*
- *Challenge your students to set goals around throwing multiple tossables. How many can they throw with how many throws and catches in a row?*
- *Have them think of their own variations.*

> ✓ **Safety Check**
>
> *Be sure to use objects that are relatively light and soft.*

Secret Agent

Estimated Time

15 minutes

Description:

Secret Agent is a fun activity in which students explore the "Be Safe" value as it relates to influence.

Learning Themes:

- Demonstrate an understanding of each of the core Full Values.
- Understand the difference between safe and risky or harmful behaviors in relationships.

Props:

None

Setup:

Find an open space free of obstacles.

Framing:

"People can sometimes make us feel safe or unsafe. What are the reasons for that? Is it the role they have? Is it something they do?"

Procedure:

1. Ask each student to look around the circle and select a guardian angel without letting anyone know who that person is. They are not to show or tell anyone, including their selected guardian angel.

2. Secondly, ask each student to select a secret agent, using the same guidelines as above.

3. The object of the activity is for each student to keep his or her guardian angel physically between him or her self and his or her secret agent! Give a physical demonstration of what that looks like.

4. Activity starts, the entire group is maneuvering about simultaneously attempting to be in this configuration.

 Tip:

This is a good activity in which to introduce the concept of "time out" or simply "Freeze." (Use whatever language suits your program. Some programs, for example, use "time out" to mean one student spends some time one-on-one with a counselor, and this is not that). You or a student can yell "Freeze" whenever an activity feels unsafe. Everyone should stop the action, circle up and discuss the problem and make a plan to fix it.

5. At the end of each round, have students thank their guardian angels and secret agents.

6. Play another or multiple rounds asking students to choose new guardian angels and secret agents for each round.

Reflection:

- How did you stay safe in this activity? Can anyone share an example of how you kept yourself or others safe?

- What will this group need to do to stay safe during class or group activities?

- Think about a person in your life who acts as your guardian angel. Who is that person who makes you feel safe? Does anyone want to share how that person makes you feel safe with the group?

- Think of a person in your life who acts as a secret agent. How does that person make you feel unsafe?

- Was anyone surprised at how they felt about their guardian angel or secret agent even though those people hadn't really done anything to make them safe or unsafe?

- Did knowing you could freeze the action help you feel safer?

Tip:

This is a great place to give an example of how you saw students keeping each other safe. Did they give each other verbal heads up, take a "time out," etc?

Tip:

Sometimes you will ask a question and no one will want to talk. That is OK. Be comfortable with silence and give your students time to think. Let their body language tell you when they're ready for the next question.

Variation

Ask the group to stop the action. Move one or two people, and then ask the group to reposition themselves. This is a great illustration of how the behavior of only a couple of people can impact an entire group. Ask your students to think about how easily someone can make something safe or unsafe. Explore this and ask them for examples.

 Additional Thoughts

Bumpers up may not be needed, but remind your students to be aware of each other and keep one another safe. You may want to require that students walk during the first round.

Pairs Tag

Estimated Time

15 minutes

Description:
Pairs Tag is a vigorous group activity that enables students to help each other Be Safe.

Learning Themes:
- Demonstrate an understanding of each of the core Full Values.
- Explore the impact of positive decision making on team performance.

Props:
None

Setup:
Create a large open space with four cones to mark the boundaries.

Framing:
"We are going to be facing some challenges together. To do that, we need to figure out ways of working together that are safe. Sometimes what we think is helping helps and sometimes it gets in the way."

Procedure:
1. Have students congregate within the boundaries.
2. Ask students to find partners and stand next to their partners.
3. Tell the class, "We are going to play a fun tag activity in which each partnership needs to come up with a way that they can demonstrate helping others be safe. We will do this by making a gesture and using words to go with that gesture – it should be a gesture that you use together. For example, I might tap someone on the shoulder (demonstrate that) and say 'Are you OK?' to show checking in on safety."
4. Give them a couple of minutes to figure what their partnership's expression of safety will be and how they will model it.
5. When the class is ready, have them come back to a circle. Ask the partners to show the rest of the class their expressions of safety by going around the circle.
6. Now comes the tag activity. Ask the partners to decide who will be the "tagger." Explain that the person who is "tagger" will chase only their partner.
7. When a partner is tagged, that person will stop wherever they are and perform the expression of safety the pair developed in Step 3, to the count of ten.

8. This person is now the "tagger" and can begin chasing his or her partner after performing an expression of safety so the original tagger better get out of there fast!

9. Partners switch back and forth for the duration of the activity.

Reflection:

1. What was it like to tag your partner and then be tagged?

2. What strategies did you and your partner come up with that helped you to play the activity?

3. What might get in the way of being helpful to your peers?

4. How does the Full Value concept of Being Here connect to Being Safe? If needed: Can we Be Safe if we aren't Being Here?

5. What are some ways to Be Safe in your daily life? Here in school/program?

 Additional Thoughts

Do not allow players to crouch behind other team members as this can result in collisions.

Out of Kilter

Description:
Out of Kilter is a fairly active pair and then small group activity in which students rely on each other to Be Safe.

Learning Themes:
- Understand and describe healthy relationships.
- Identify methods used to recognize and avoid threatening situations.

Props:
- Boundary markers (rope, cones, spot markers or the like)

 Estimated Time

15 minutes

Setup:
Create a fairly large open space in your classroom. Be sure to stay away from hard surfaces and protruding edges. Define the boundaries with polyspots, traffic cones, rope, etc.

Framing:
"Our friends can either bring us down or help hold us up. Finding balance in our lives while supporting our friends is challenging!"

Procedure:

1. Ask students to find a partner who appears to be their "total opposite."

2. Explain to the class that this is an activity about balance, yours and your partner's. The object is to always be physically unbalanced.

3. Tell the partners to grab one another's hands or wrists, lean backwards, away from each other, until they find that if it were not for the support of their partner, they would topple over.

4. Explain that while they are in the process of putting themselves out of balance, their partner is doing the same.

5. Tell the partners to move around a bit and try different positions, all the while regaining a sense of balance to the point of imbalance. As they get more comfortable with one another, they can get a bit more daring.

6. Now find another pair and make your duo a quadruple. Be careful! Four unbalanced people can lead to a heap of falling bodies. If everyone's still engaged, have the groups switch partners for more balanced/unbalanced experiences.

7. Again, the task is to create a point of imbalance that won't work without the support of your partners. If you feel that you are going to fall, take a step backward/forward.

Reflection:

Reflection Activity:

1. Remind the group that we have been talking about the importance of relationships in being safe. Have the groups of four brainstorm, describe and write down their thoughts about the following:

    •   when family and/or peer relationships are in balance and

    •   when they can get out of balance and can/have become unsafe.

    •   ways to keep relationships from becoming dangerously out of balance – unsafe.

2. Have the groups of four come back to the large group and share their responses.

3. Observe that during the activity, it seemed as though it took a lot of trust and support to take different kinds of risks. (Give examples, if possible.) How can peers trust and support one another as they face the many challenges of being in safe relationships?

Stepping Stones

Description:

This active initiative helps students to understand the role of goal setting in behavior or letting go of negative behaviors.

Learning Themes:

- Describe how one's choices and decisions impact the achievement of goals.
- Describe or demonstrate the benefits of positive and challenging goals.
- Demonstrate ability to notice what gets in our way when setting goals.

Props:

- Stepping Stones Kit*
- Boundary markers

Estimated Time

40 minutes

Setup:

1. Create a distance that your students must travel across. It should be a large rectangular area. With boundary markers at each corner, some rope, etc, mark a start and a finish line.

2. Randomly, not in straight row, place stepping stones (foam squares, carpet squares or the like) between the start and finish lines. The stones will be a path which your students will traverse from the start line to the finish line. The stepping stones should be no further than three feet (the measurement not the body part) apart. Some can be placed nearer to one another and therefore easier to traverse and others placed further apart and therefore harder.

Tip:

The distances between the stepping stones are recommendations. If your group is able to focus and willing to take care of each other, you can make it more challenging. If your group is not ready for this, make it easier. This activity should be challenging, but doable.

Framing:

"Another value that keeps us growing is the ability to Let Go and Move On. This requires that we first identify what we need to let go of ourselves as well as helping others identify what they need to let go of. Think about behaviors you have – we all have them – that are slowing you down or stopping you from moving forward and achieving your goals. Those are behaviors you want to let go of, right? Once your entire team has arrived at the other side, you can share what you are giving up."

Procedure:

1. Every student must cross the marked area from the start line to the finish.

2. No one may touch the ground; students may only stand on the stepping stones.

---

* Available from Project Adventure

3. Players must remain in contact with the stones at all times, once original contact has been made. If a stone is left unattended (no one is touching it), it is lost. That means that if the leader sees a stone that is not touched at any time, you should take it out of the crossing area so students can't use it.

4. If any student touches the ground for any reason, the entire class must go back to the start. You can put the lost stones back or not or put some back as fits the level of challenge for your group.

Reflection:

1. As a team, how did you feel about how you worked together to accomplish this task?

2. Were there times when you lost focus and lost a stepping stone?

3. Did you feel like you really let your team down?

4. You were asked to identify something you need to let go of. Share what you are letting go of.

5. So, is that a goal of yours, to let (whatever they identified in their previous answer) go? How can we help you? What do you need to achieve your goal?

Variations

Make it more challenging:

• *Blindfold some or all students.*
• *No verbal communication.*
• *Give the students the stones and have them problem solve how to place the stones.*

Make it less challenging:

• *Only the student who touches the ground, not the whole group, goes back to the end of the line.*
• *The foam squares could be labeled with group goals, resources that will help them in life (i.e., AA meetings or sponsors, their parents, a special teacher, etc) or Full Value traits and reflection could include a discussion of how those things help you move on.*
• *Students could label an index card with one or two things they are letting go of and leave them at the start. Keep these labeled index cards and return to them during the reflection piece. This will help to increase the concreteness of this activity.*

Human Camera

Description:
This quiet partner trust activity enables students to explore what Being Honest means to them.

Learning Themes:
- Define and demonstrate the ability to be honest.
- Define and demonstrate the ability to give and receive trust.

Props:
None

Estimated Time

40 minutes

Setup:
Ask students to form pairs, preferably choosing someone with whom they are less familiar.

Framing:
"Each of you will have an opportunity to be a gifted photographer as well as an expensive camera. As the photographer, you will be looking around the _____ (wherever they can safely explore at your program site – it is OK if it is just a classroom) to capture snapshots that in some way represent being honest."

Procedure:

1. The photographer's task is to capture three different photographs each representing honesty. Their partner will act as the Human Camera.

2. Give everyone about ten minutes to walk around the area to locate their three snapshots.

3. Once the group has returned, have the pairs designate who will be the first photographer and who will be the first camera.

4. The first photographer will lead the Human Camera to his or her first snapshot. The Camera is to keep his or her eyes closed while being led.

5. Once the photographer is in front of the snapshot, he or she should carefully position the camera's head so that, when he or she opens her eyes, they will be looking directly at the designated photograph. Once the Camera is properly positioned, the photographer can take the picture.

6. A picture is taken by gently tapping the shoulder of the Camera. When this is done, the Camera quickly opens and closes his or her eyes to get a snapshot view of what is in front of him or her.

Tip:

This is another opportunity for students to demonstrate that they are capable...capable of safely leading others.

7. Repeat this for the other two photographs.

8. The partners can either change roles now, or begin the discussion below about the photographs before moving to the next three photographs. Both sequences work well.

9. Repeat the above steps.

Reflection:

Option 1: Reflection Activity:

1. Remaining in original pairs, have each camera share what they saw in the three different photographs and their interpretations. Have the photographers then clarify what they were hoping to capture.

2. The pairs should then choose two shots to present to the group – one taken by each photographer.

3. Then, have them share with the whole group.

4. Ask questions and allow students to ask questions as they naturally emerge.

Option 2: Questions for Reflection:

1. Was there anything your photographer could have done to make you feel safer?

2. In this activity, did it feel like you were taking more physical or emotional risks?

3. What were ways that you were honest with your partner?

4. What are some examples of how trust was needed?

Moon Ball

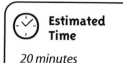

Estimated Time

20 minutes

> ### Description:
> Moon Ball is an activity that sets the stage for students to practice setting and achieving goals while having fun.
>
> ### Learning Themes:
> - Describe or demonstrate the benefits of positive and challenging goals.
> - Support each other in achieving goals and making decisions.
> - Know from whom and how to get assistance.
>
> ### Props:
> - Large inflatable balls

Setup:
Ask students to stand in a circle and have one or two large inflatable balls available. An open space or gymnasium is best.

Framing:
"What are some goals you have set or achieved? We all have hopes or dreams. Goals are those little steps we need to take to make our dreams happen. Let's practice setting goals so we can make our dreams happen. As a team, we want to set a goal for how many consecutive hits we can make to keep this moon ball up in the air, with no one hitting the ball twice in a row. We know that goals have to be reasonable but not too easy. What do you think our goal should be for the number of times we can hit the moon ball up in the air as a group?"

 Tip:

*Try to be non-judgmental about the goals. Your students will likely figure out on their own that an easy goal is not something they will feel good about achieving or that too ambitious a goal is frustrating. If not, help them come to that conclusion during your reflection discussion. **Bottom Line:** They will learn more through experience.*

Procedure:
1. First give your students the opportunity for a little experimentation. Let them toss the ball in the air while counting the number of consecutive hits – without someone hitting it twice in a row. Let them get a feel for how they will do before they set a goal.

Tip:

Let your students count hits and assess their goal achievement.

Tip:

Take a break! Play a tag or other activity just for fun throughout. Balance your students' needs for play and processing of the experience.

2. Then your students need to set a goal of how many hits they can keep the ball in the air for without it being hit twice in a row by someone or hitting the ground.

3. Once the ball is in the air – the students should start hitting and the group and you should start counting.

4. Each time the ball hits the ground or someone hits it twice in a row, pick up the ball and ask the students if they want to change their goal. After they have agreed to keep their goal or have changed their goal, start the ball again.

5. The second level of Moon Ball is to ask the class to do as many consecutive hits in a row, with no one hitting the ball a second time until everyone has hit the ball at least once.

6. This is an activity students like to play repeatedly, so let them if you have time!

Reflection:

1. Do you feel that our goal was too easy or too hard? Explain.

2. Do you think it was important to reevaluate your goals? If so, why?

3. What did it feel like when we had to start over because the ball hit the ground?

4. How did we help each other reach our group goal?

5. What happens when you set an individual goal but don't make it?

6. Who can help you reach your program/school goals?

7. What are some strategies we can use to help each other reach our goals? (Capture these on flipchart paper to take back and display in classroom).

Variations

• *Have two balls in play at the same time.*
• *Record the goals and attempts on flip chart paper.*

Welded Ankles

Description:

In this activity, students experience balancing the need to take care of themselves while taking care of others.

Learning Themes:

- Learn to work together to achieve a common goal or task.
- Define and identify ways of caring for and helping self and others.
- Learn to express one's feelings verbally.

Props:

- Spot or other marker
- Pen or pencils, one for each student
- A piece of paper or index card for each student

Estimated Time

15 minutes

Setup:

1. Have students line up with their ankles touching.
2. Place a spot marker (or any marker) a quarter of a turn away. If the end of the line is pointing to 12 on an imaginary clock, the marker should be at 3 or 9.

Framing:

"As a community, we have the value of Caring for Self and Others. In this activity, we will experience what it is like to take care of each other and understand the complexities of everyone's needs in the group. While you participate in this activity, be thinking of how we can take care of each other while still taking care of ourselves."

Procedure:

1. Each person must remain in physical contact by ankles throughout the entire activity.
2. The group must turn one quarter of a circle by moving the entire line.
3. If they lose contact with one another's ankle(s), they should start over. (Or, they could count the number of times they lose contact.)

Reflection:

Reflection Activity:

1. Divide the student group into pairs.
2. Give each pair a pen or pencil and a piece of paper.

3. Ask each partnership to discuss and write five examples of how they took care of others during this activity.

4. Ask each partnership to discuss and write five examples of how they took care of themselves.

5. Ask the pairs to report what they came up with to the larger group and give time for other students and you to ask questions.

6. Post the papers.

Variations

• *Turn every other person in the opposite direction.*
• *Do the activity blindfolded or sightless.*

Dead Ant Tag

Estimated Time

20 minutes

Tip:

Always read the entire activity before beginning it! Don't do it if it seems inappropriate. For example, this activity might not be appropriate for students who have been victims of sexual abuse. (See the variation below for a way of playing that might be suitable.)

Description:
Dead Ant Tag is a vigorous activity in which students help each other and explore Caring for Self and Others.

Learning Themes:
• Define and identify ways of caring for and helping self and others.
• Demonstrate an understanding of each of the core Full Values.

Props:
• 5 Hula™ type hoops

Setup:
Spread the five hoops around a playing field, gym or other open area.

Framing:
"Sometimes when we help others, we can help ourselves. Let's see how this works in a fun activity of tag."

Procedure:
1. Determine who will act as the poison (Raid™). Have one Raid for every 12 or so students. These students will hold a fleece ball to identify who they are.

The ball is for identification, not for throwing, so a bandanna or the like will work equally well.

2. The remaining students are ants.

3. The Raid's objective is to tag as many ants as possible.

4. Review the basics of a safe tag: gentle and on the back and shoulder.

5. Explain that when ants are tagged, they are to lie down on their backs and put their legs and feet in the air. Then they yell: "Dead ant, dead ant, dead ant, dead ant!" to get the attention of other ants who can help save them.

6. The injured ant begins to get revived when four other ants come and carefully take hold of each of his/her limbs. The four ants complete the rescue by carefully carrying the injured ant into the "hospital." The hospitals are the hula hoops. When bringing a dead ant to the hospital, students can make the sounds of an ambulance.

7. Once the injured ant is inside the hoop, they are cured!

8. Ants that are busy taking care of an injured ant are immune from getting sprayed with Raid.

9. Repeat with new Raid cans, as time and interest permits.

Reflection:

1. Did you help bring anyone to the hospital? Did anyone help you?

2. How did you care for yourself and others in this activity?

3. How does it feel to help others?

4. When you were helping others, how did you help yourself?

5. Can you think of a time, outside of this activity, when you helped yourself by helping others? (Facilitator: If needed, give a hint – "Sometimes you feel better about yourself when you help others.")

6. Can you name some ways we can care for others in our classroom/program? Can you name some ways we can care for ourselves?

 Tip:

Try not to finish an activity with the group not feeling successful. Reflect in a way that highlights their attributes and accomplishments. Sometimes this means they didn't accomplish the task of the activity, but honestly feel good about their effort.

Variation

If having students carry each other by the limbs does not seem appropriate for your group, try the following variation: Instead of injured ants being cured by being carried to the "hospital," they are spontaneously cured when they have one ant touching each of their limbs.

7, 11, 21

Estimated Time

20 minutes

Description:

7, 11, 21 is a Rock, Paper, Scissors type activity to introduce and delve into the Full Value of Let Go and Move On.

Learning Themes:

- Define and/or demonstrate the ability to compromise.
- Demonstrate an understanding of each of the core Full Values.

Props:

None

Framing:

"Sometimes people just get stuck. They expect things to happen one way and they happen another. Or, they keep doing the same thing over and over expecting things to turn out differently. I think you'll see what I mean as we do this activity."

Procedure:

1. Ask each student to find a partner.

2. Explain that this activity is very much like Rock, Paper, Scissors in that someone will count to three and each member of the group will display their fingers but instead of rock, paper or scissors, they will be trying to come up with the sum of a predetermined number.

3. The partners should turn back to back and on your count of three (or ready, set, go etc.), they should turn around holding up their fingers in a way that together they think they will have seven fingers. The pair shouldn't discuss what numbers they will show on their fingers beforehand.

4. Give the partnerships one minute to see how many times they can come up with the number seven between them. For example, one student displays three fingers and the other student displays four.

5. Ask how many pairs got seven fingers.

6. Ask the students to get into teams of three. Same rules apply except now the goal is 11.

7. Ask the students to get into teams of five. Same rules apply except now the goal is 21.

8. Finally, ask the students to get into teams of seven. Each team is now going for the number 30.

Reflection:

1. How challenging was it to throw number 7? 11? 21? 30?

2. How did the different number of people in your groups change your decisions as to how many fingers to display?

3. What qualities did it take to work together?

4. What kind of compromise occurred within the groups?

5. Was it some people's strategy to throw the same number of fingers every time so the others in their group would know what they were doing? How did that work?

6. How hard was it to figure out what others in your group were doing? Was it frustrating not to be able to talk and strategize?

7. Do you want to let go of any of the behaviors you used during this activity? Are you holding on to any behaviors or issues you should be letting go of?

8. How does this relate to our value of Letting Go and Moving On?

Variation

Teams can compete against each other in a relay race. Make stations (simply place chairs, polyspots, etc. at equal intervals to represent each station) at which teams have to throw each number. Teams need to throw each number using the rules above before moving to the next station. They can throw the numbers as a team or you can ask them to divide into the groupings described above.

Bear, Salmon and Mosquito

Estimated Time

20 minutes

Description:

Bear, Salmon and Mosquito is an energetic activity that helps students to understand their responses to conflict.

Learning Themes:
- Demonstrate self-awareness through the expression of thoughts and feelings.
- Understand conflict and reactions to conflict.

Props:
- 15-20 foot length of rope
- Cones / Markers

Setup:

1. Place the long rope in the center of a large, open space.
2. Create two safety zones by placing two cones on each side of the center line, about 20 yards away from it.

Framing:

"This activity will give us the opportunity to practice our fight or flight response and to understand how we anticipate and manage conflict. We will be working in two small groups and this center line is our point of conflict."

Procedure:

1. Divide the students into two small groups.
2. Tell the class that they need to know how to represent three creatures: bear, salmon and mosquito.
3. Tell them as you demonstrate how to create each creature. "Bears are very tall, with their hands straight up over their head and give a great big 'ROOOAAAR.'"
4. "Salmon are formed by placing your two hands together in prayer fashion, pointing away from your body and then swishing them forward while making a swooshing water sound."
5. "Mosquitoes are formed by spreading your arms out to your side, wiggling your fingers while making a loud buzzing noise."
6. Bears eat salmon, salmon eat mosquitoes and mosquitoes bite bears on the nose. This is important. Have the group repeat it back to you and review with physical demonstrations of what chases what.

7. The goal is for each small group to win members from the other group.

8. Each small group goes back to their safety line (the area 20 feet away from the center line you marked with cones) and decides quietly among themselves what creature they would like to be. The group then comes back to the center-line where at the count of three, all members show the decided-upon bear, salmon or mosquito.

9. The group that shows the creature that eats or bites the other becomes the chasers and the other group, the runners. The runners try to run past their cones to safety without being tagged. For example, Bears would chase Salmon, Salmon chase Mosquitoes and Mosquitoes chase Bears.

10. If the runners are tagged, they become members of the other team, and each team gets another planning session.

11. If each side shows the same creature, students shake hands, return to their small groups and try again.

12. Ask students to try to identify what they are thinking or feeling right before they show their creature and immediately after.

13. Play a few rounds or until most of the group is on one side.

Reflection:

1. Can you describe what you were feeling when you stepped up to the line to show your creature?

2. Can you describe what you were feeling when the other team showed their creature and you had to instantly decide whether to chase or be chased?

3. Can you describe what you were feeling when you showed your creature and it was the same as the other side's?

4. How do you think these feelings relate to our responses to conflict?

5. Do you feel your response was helpful or harmful in this activity? How might your reactions connect to your behaviors in the classroom?

6. Can you describe some ways to avoid, diminish or stop threatening situations that may come up in our classroom?

Section II:
Personal Goals and Behavioral Change

This section will deepen students' understandings of personal goals as they relate to behavioral change. Specifically, students will create measurable goals that will promote positive behavioral change.

More on Setting Goals: The process of goal setting is a key element to an adventure program. It is also key to fostering resiliency among at-risk youth. Research has consistently shown that having a sense of purpose, which includes being able to set and attain goals, is a significant way for resiliency to be manifested.[6] Helping your students learn how to set and attain goals will be one of the fundamental skills for success that you will give them. Goal setting requires the ability to see what needs to be accomplished to attain a goal and then follow those steps to the goal's achievement. Making good, positive choices and then pursuing them is the action of goal setting. Goal setting is another behavior/concept that teachers/staff need to model.

Students need to set their own goals within the context of the goals of the program and the Full Value Contract. They may need your help ensuring that these goals: 1) can be reached in a relatively short period of time, 2) will promote the attainment of long-term goals and 3) have a payoff for achieving goals that is perceived by the students to be real and valuable.

Students will state what each goal looks like and what the payoff will be if they meet it. Goal sheets help to make student goals concrete and measurable. You will find goal sheets in the Appendix.

The SMART Way to Set Goals

SMART Goals

SMART goal setting is an acronym that contains a handy set of guidelines to help in the construction of goals.

Specific: The goal is easily understood and stated by all members of the community with no alternatives and no "outs." If the goal is changed, it must be negotiated. Goals can be added, but not at the expense of the original goal.

Measurable: The goal has time (completion date), and quantity (how much of it) measurements.

Achievable: The goal must have a reasonable chance of success. Setting impossible goals can be a way to avoid responsibility for them.

Relevant: Is it important to pursue this goal? Is it a goal that has already been achieved, and is therefore not a challenge? Can other goals be built upon this one?

Trackable: Can you check in and tell if you have completed all or part of it? Vague goals cannot be tracked.

6.Benard, Bonnie; *Fostering Resiliency in Children*; ERIC Digest; 1995

Talk with your program administrators and staff about the exact structure of setting and monitoring goals for your program. One structure might be to set a goal (for the program or school, not home, etc.) on the first day of your program week. Do a quick goal check-in at the end of each program day. This might be done by saying, "Using your thumb as an indicator with thumbs down being 'I didn't do anything to accomplish my goal today' and thumbs up being 'I totally accomplished my goal today,' show us how you think you did. Remember, you can use the whole range between thumbs up and thumbs down." Allow time for reflection on how they did. Question people whose thumbs are up or down if you disagree with them. Be sure to take issue using concrete examples of what happened in the program today. Let students who want to take a minute or two to discuss how they did.

Activities:

- Chicken Baseball
- Goal Mapping
- How Do You Do?
- I'm OK, You OK? Tag
- Pathway to the Life I Want
- Target Practice
- Visioning Path

Chicken Baseball

Estimated Time

25 minutes

Tip:

Allow teams to call time-outs. Calling a time out for both teams during play can accentuate goal revision and evaluation.

Description:

In this fun, moderately-paced activity, students begin to identify the numerous skills needed to set a goal.

Learning Themes:

- Describe the skills needed to set healthy personal and/or group goals.
- Demonstrate an ability to evaluate and revise personal and/or group goals.

Props:

- Rubber Chicken

Setup:

1. Find an open space – a gym or playing field works well.
2. Divide your class into two teams. Teams can range from 5 to 15 or so students.

Framing:

"You'd be surprised at how often we use planning, revising and other skills we need for goal setting without thinking about it. We're going to play a baseball activity. This version of baseball has some similarities to traditional baseball; there are two teams and you can score runs, but that's where the similarities end."

Procedure:

1. One team (team A) is the "infield." The other team (team B) is the "outfield." Team A starts by throwing the rubber chicken anywhere in the designated play area (the entire gym, or a whole soccer field, for example).
2. Once the chicken has been thrown, team B runs toward it and forms a single-file line behind it. The first person in line picks up the chicken and passes it through his or her legs to the person directly behind, who passes it over his or her head. This over-under passing pattern continues until the chicken has reached the end of the line and the last student in line yells, "Stop!"
3. Meanwhile, team A is scoring runs. A run is scored every time one student from team A runs around all of the team A group members. Teams keep track of their own scores, which are cumulative from inning to inning.
4. As soon as team B yells, "Stop," the last student in line throws the chicken to any other spot in the designated play area. Team B then begins to score runs as team A lines up and starts passing the chicken.

5. The activity is over after five innings, or when you determine that it's time to stop.

6. If the chicken goes out of bounds (into the bleachers, for example), the team that has thrown it gets to throw again.

7. Take a moment and set a quick goal for yourself in this activity.

Reflection:

- Did each team create plans that helped them be more successful?

- How did you revise your plan?

- What were your individual goals? How did you stick to your goals? Or not?

- Was it hard to make changes on the fly or did it just come naturally?

- What were some of the feelings that came up for you when you worked together toward your goal of scoring more runs than the other team?

- What were some learnings about setting appropriate goals in this activity that we can take back to the unit/classroom/program?

Tip:

You don't always need to connect the dots. By giving your students the opportunity to do so, you are allowing them to develop their ability to have insight. It is yet another way you empower them.

Additional Thoughts

- *Point out the boundaries to students and remove any obstacles.*

- *Emphasize that only one student should be scoring runs at a time; otherwise there could be collisions.*

- *A rubber chicken really does work best. If you use a ball, it tends to roll and slow down the activity.*

- *Add a rule that requires students to choose a different runner to score runs for every inning, so as not to overtire the student who is always last to arrive to the remainder of the team.*

Goal Mapping

Estimated Time

15 minutes

Tip:

This is a good activity to address individuals' beliefs about themselves and their abilities. Helping them see their potential and influence will positively impact their self efficacy.

Description:

In this worksheet-driven activity, students begin to understand the roles of desire, ability, need and benefits in goal-setting.

Learning Themes:

- Describe or demonstrate the benefits of positive and challenging goals.

Setup:

Give each student a copy of the Goal Mapping worksheet.

Framing:

"Sometimes when we set goals, we say the things we think we should say without really thinking about the benefits of achieving that goal. For example, students often say they have a goal of staying focused in class, without thinking through the benefits of achieving that goal, e.g., getting more done, getting better grades and earning more respect for their peers and teachers."

Procedure:

1. Hand out worksheets to each student.
2. Explain the following: Start with the central idea of what you Desire to change – Write it in the big circle. This becomes the goal to focus on. It is the central idea.
3. Choose one of the lines that extend from that first circle and make another circle. Write inside that circle the **Benefits** from making this change.
4. Do the same task with your **Abilities** to make this change. Think about what might get in the way. What are your assets that will help you to make this change and overcome things that get in the way.
5. Under the box that indicates **Need: Reasons to Change**, describe your reasons to focus on this goal.

Additional Thoughts

Have the students hold onto this goal map and revisit either in groups, partnerships or individual reflection.

Consider revisiting and revising this goal map on a periodic basis.

Reflection:

1. Who wants to share their goal?

2. Does drawing out your goal for change, benefits and ability help you to understand it better? How or why does it do this?

3. How does this goal apply to the classroom/unit?

4. Do we need to add anything to this map?

How Do You Do?

> **Description:**
>
> In this fast-paced activity, students express appreciation for one another.
>
> **Learning Themes:**
> - Support each other in achieving goals and making decisions.
> - Know and appreciate one's peers.
>
> **Props:**
>
> None

Setup:

Have your group stand in a circle with one person in the middle.

Framing:

"It is important to acknowledge people all the time, but especially if you are going to help them achieve their goals."

Procedure:

1. The middle person approaches someone in the circle, looks him or her in the eye, shakes his or her hand, and says "How do you do?" The person who is approached answers "Fine, thanks!" They repeat this three times.

2. After the third handshake, the pair splits, one running in one direction around the outside of the circle, the other running in the opposite direction outside the circle

3. They will meet again about halfway around. When they do, they are to stop, shake hands, and say "How do you do?" and "Fine, thanks!" one time.

4. Next they race back to the original starting point. Whoever arrives last goes back into the middle of the circle.

5. While the runners are moving around the circle, the other students can extend their hands whenever they would like, which REQUIRES the runner to stop, make eye contact with them, shake hands and say "How do you do?" to which the runner responds, "Fine thanks." This incorporates everyone into the activity, and slows down the outside runners.

Reflection:

1. What did it feel like to be acknowledged?
2. What did it feel like to acknowledge others?
3. How was it to try to reach your goal, your spot back in the circle, and be interrupted by people looking for acknowledgement?
4. How does this happen in our program/classroom?

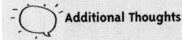 **Additional Thoughts**

• *Ask the runners to move at a safe speed. This may be at a fast walk if the ground is wet or the circle is very small.*

• *Remind people that they must do ONE handshake when they meet. This helps to prevent collisions.*

• *Warn circle people to put their hands out early enough so as not to hit runners or be hit by the runners.*

I'm OK, You OK? Tag

Description:

This tag activity enables students to identify ways in which they can support one another.

Learning Themes:

• Support each other in achieving goals and making decisions.
• Define and identify ways of caring for and helping self and others.
• Demonstrate an ability to appropriately express one's needs and emotions.

Props:

None

Setup:
You will need an open space where the group can circle up and move around.

Tip:

Use an example that works for you. It doesn't have to be a party or dance – maybe it is lunch at school or an after-school event.

Framing:
"One strategy for achieving our goals is to have a "buddy" and a plan. Your friends can be sources of support during times when achieving goals might seem hard. This activity will help you to practice finding one another amid the chaos that we sometimes experience during life."

Procedure:

1. Ask students to find partners and form a circle inside the open space, standing next to their partners.

2. Tell the students they are going to play a fun tag activity with their partners.

3. In other words, tell them, "Just you and your partner will be chasing one another, but everyone will do that at the same time."

4. Ask the group to imagine that they are at a big dance or party with their friend and they have agreed to check in with one another every so often to make sure that they are both OK.

5. Explain that this tag activity represents the party and that when you tag your partner, you say, "Are you OK?" Your partner says "I'm OK," and counts to ten, while you get away.

6. Tell students that once they are tagged, their partner becomes the tagger and will chase them after they count to ten. When they find their partner, they tag that person and say, "Are you OK?" That person says, "I'm OK," counts to ten and repeats the process.

7. Remind students that once they have answered the questions, the person who is now being chased should move away from his/her partner while that person is counting to ten.

8. Have each partnership decide who will start as the tagger and begin.

Reflection:

1. How did it feel to make contact (tag) with your support buddy throughout the activity?

2. How can your goal buddy be helpful and someone you seek out versus someone you run away from?

3. How did the chaos of the setting affect your ability to make good decisions or not run into other people?

4. What ways did you stay connected to your partner even when you were separated or running away from them?

5. If you really were at a party or dance, what are some ways you could let your friends know you are not OK?

Pathway to the Life I Want

Estimated Time

40 minutes

> **Description:**
> This moderately-active group initiative enables students to envision the life they want.
>
> **Learning Themes:**
> - Describe a positive future for one's self.
> - Describe how one's choices and decisions impact the achievement of goals.
> - Explain how mistakes can be learning experiences and used to help achieve one's goals.
>
> **Props:**
> - 30 spot markers
> - Drawing markers
> - Masking tape
> - Optional: graph paper

Setup:

1. Prepare the spot markers by putting an X, using the masking tape, on the numbered side of each spot marker that is not on the pathway. Either leave the appropriate numbers (if using spot markers from your Keypunch set) on your spot markers or use masking tape to number them – as in the diagram below.

2. You will need to create the "Pathway to the Life I Want" that your students will follow. To help you create this pathway, map it out on a piece of paper (graph paper works well) and devise a route that will use 30 spots and begin at the entrance side of the area and end at the exit side. Don't share this with your students!

3. Lay your spots out, numbered or Xed side down, in a five by six grid.

4. Solutions can involve forward, side or backward movements. Diagonal moves or moves that skip rows are not allowed.

5. The more moves you create in your solution, the more difficult the activity will be. If you want a challenging Pathway you could use only 5 X spots and 25 numbered spots.

ENTRANCE ⇨

1	2	X	16	17	18
X	3	4	15	14	X
X	6	5	X	13	X
X	7	X	11	12	X
X	8	9	10	X	X

⇨ EXIT

Framing:

"Living the life we want involves, in part, accessing quality information. Creating a plan for the life we want involves making and implementing positive choices and setting and achieving goals. This activity will help us to understand the consequences of making bad choices and identify skills we need to lead the life we want."

Procedure:

1. Tell the group that the challenge for this activity is to find the Pathway to Life I Want. This is accomplished by discovering the correct sequence of steps to get one person from the entrance to the exit.

2. To do this they will select a spot, turn it over and read the number to determine if it is a positive choice. If it is a positive choice (as represented only by the next number – if four was the last overturned and correct number, only five would be a positive choice), step on the spot and repeat the process with another spot within range. If they have made a bad choice, they must exit the Pathway exactly the way they entered.

3. Only a positive choice spot would remain turned over, students must turn their bad choices back with number/X side down before exiting the Pathway.

4. One person at a time is allowed to enter the Pathway. If they make positive choices, they may continue.

5. People on the Pathway may only move forward, backward or sideways. Diagonal moves or moves that skip a row are not allowed.

6. After the framing, group members may position themselves anywhere around the Pathway to assist the person on the Pathway and to observe. No verbal or written communication is allowed with the person on the Pathway. Nonverbal communication is allowed.

 Tip:

Ask for a real life example of achievement of a goal. Map out the steps on a flip chart or white board. Identify where learning from mistakes occurred along the way.

7. The person on the Pathway should not be touched.

8. The group will rotate turns so that no person enters the grid for a second time until everyone has entered once.

9. Remind the group that they need to be careful not to duplicate bad choices.

10. The activity ends when the group is able to get one person through the pathway.

Reflection:

1. What were the steps you took to find the pathway to the life you want?

2. How did you feel about trying to find the path even though you were set back by bad choices?

3. So, you reached your goal despite mistakes. How does that relate to your own life?

4. Did anyone have a small goal when they took their turn, for example, a goal of turning over one or two positive choices? If so, do you feel like that helped you and/or your team? How?

5. How do you think making choices relates to achieving goals?

6. What skills did you use to stay on the path?

7. How can you use these skills to maintain your own plan for graduating this program? Improving grades? Getting a job?

> **Tip:**
>
> *Give your students time to talk. If they come up with a powerful discussion thread, explore it! The activity will be more powerful than if you just stay with the questions here.*

Variations

• *Have the only "map" of the pathway be your diagram. Students have to commit to memory the right and wrong steps through the pathway. You can also add that everyone has to make it through but they can use verbal communication and coach a teammate through the pathway.*

• *Have a student create the pathway for the group.*

Target Practice

Description:

In this activity, students practice writing goals. There is a worksheet in the Appendix that provides the structure for the activity.

Learning Themes:

- Describe the skills needed to set healthy personal and/or group goals.
- Demonstrate an ability to evaluate and revise personal and/or group goals.
- Describe or demonstrate the benefits of positive and challenging goals.

Props:

- Target Practice Worksheet

 Estimated Time

20 minutes

Setup:

Each student needs a personal copy of the Target Practice worksheet.

Framing:

"We have been talking about how important it is to set goals. Let's get really specific about how you do that, so we can!"

Procedure:

1. Before handing out the worksheets, give the students the following example of how to be specific with their goals.

   Include:

   The task or goal you want to accomplish
   How it will be measured – what will it look like when it is done (standard)
   How long it will take to accomplish (time span)

   Example:

   I will honor others' personal individual spaces with fewer than five prompts by the end of the week.

   I will _____ with _____ by _____.
             (task)   (standard)   (time span)

2. Assist students in streamlining their goals and relating them to individual treatment plans.

 Tip:

Help students make the goals specific. For example, if someone writes, "communicate better," help to rewrite as "use I statements" or "let others finish thought/sentence before speaking," etc.

Reflection:

Reflection Activity:

Lay out ropes on the ground in concentric circles in the same formation as the worksheet – a target. Let the students report out to their peers as they move from the outside rope to the bull's eye.

Questions for Discussion:

1. Who wants to share their goal?
2. How hard was it to be specific with the standard and time span?
3. How can we help each other to accomplish these goals?
4. What will we do when we accomplish these goals?

Visioning Path

Estimated Time

25 minutes

Tip:

This is a great activity to model with your students. Let them know, by example, that people always have dreams, beliefs and goals and they are, usually, evolving.

Description:

In this art activity, students begin to envision the life they want and how they will accomplish it.

Learning Themes:

- Describe the skills needed to set healthy personal and/or group goals.
- Demonstrate an ability to evaluate and revise personal and/or group goals.
- Describe a positive future for one's self.

Props:

- 2 sheets of art paper
- Drawing markers
- Tape
- 10 note/index cards

Setup:

None

Framing:

"Think about where you want to be in six months, a positive way your life could be. We are going to describe that and then think about some steps that will get us there."

Procedure:

1. Give your students one piece of art paper and ask them to draw their life right now (using words or pictures).

2. When they are finished, give them a second piece of paper and ask them to draw how they would like their life to be in six months.

3. When they are finished, tape the first drawing (life right now) on one side of the room. It will have more visual impact if you tape/have your students tape these pictures on the same wall. Then ask your students to physically place themselves and their second picture (my positive life in six months) as far away as the goal seems from how their life is now.

4. Then give the students index cards. On each card, ask students to write one behavior they can begin that could bring them closer to their goals.

5. Using their index cards, ask students to make a path from their life as it is now to their goal life. Your students should, one at a time, make their paths by 1) reading an index card aloud, 2) placing it on the floor to represent the path to their goal life and 3) moving forward and repeating 1 and 2 until all index cards are used and they have reached their goal life.

Reflection:

1. What behavioral words did we come up with to get to our goals?

2. Are there similarities or differences among people in the group? Describe.

3. How can we help each other with these goals?

4. How far away is the beginning drawing from your goal life drawing? Does this seem realistic? What are the identifiable steps in between?

5. What are some ways you can remind yourself of your goals daily, weekly or monthly?

Variation

Have each student keep their cards on a ring and pull them off or write "complete" on them when they have accomplished the goals.

Section III:
Further Developing the Full Value Contract

The goal of this section is to continue the development of the Full Value Contract. So far, in this chapter, students have explored the six Full Values and how they might be applied in your classroom/program. Now it is time to take that important step of creating a Contract. Remember, that while the FVC creation is important, intentional and thoughtful, it can also be fun. "What do we want to be?" is a fun question to explore. Don't worry if you missed something or if things change. Your FVC is not written in stone; it is *supposed* to be a living document. As your group grows and evolves, areas of change will be identified and your Full Value Contract will need to be modified accordingly. Through the activities in this section, students will also deepen their understanding of the Full Values and how they translate to behavior.

Activities:

- Circle of Strength
- Rules? What Rules?
- Contract Garden
- Metaphor Creation
- Tower of Power
- Pie Charting
- The Being
- Create a Village

Circle of Strength

Description:

In this activity, you and your students will create your Full Value Contract.

Learning Themes:

- Demonstrate an understanding of each of the core Full Values.
- Understand and describe how the Full Value Contract can be an asset to their community.
- Describe and demonstrate what it means to be a contributing member of a Full Value community.

Props:

- Large piece of paper
- Markers
- Construction paper
- Glitter
- Feathers
- Glue
- Cut-out shapes
- Scissors

 Estimated Time

50 minutes

Setup:

None

Framing:

"We know that creating a classroom environment that is safe and challenging will help us practice and learn about being safe in the real world. We have been doing a great job of …(site behaviors from previous activities, i.e., listening to each other, cheering each other on, making sure everyone participates, etc). Let's strengthen our commitment to those behaviors by creating a circle of strength with our hands and identify specific goals for each of us to work on this semester."

Procedure:

STEP ONE: (20 minutes)

1. Have each student trace their hand on a piece of paper, cut it out, and decorate it in a way that represents who they are and what goal they have for the class.

2. If time allows, have students connect their hands into a large circle and tape or glue them to the large sheet of paper.

3. Divide the circle into six equal sections and write each of the core Full Values (Be Here, Be Safe, Be Honest, Set Goals, Care for Self and Others and Let Go and Move On) in each section.

STEP TWO: (20 minutes)

1. Gather all the students around the circle of hands and ask them to reflect on what behaviors and attitudes have been helpful to the class. In the middle of the circle of hands, have students write words describing the behaviors and attitudes in the appropriate Full Value sections.

2. Have the students write the words or draw pictures that express these positive behaviors and attitudes inside the outline of the hands.

3. Have students write words describing behaviors they don't want to see in their classroom/program community outside the circle.

4. Have students explain what they mean by the words they have chosen. Even if the words are the same, the meanings may be different for different people.

5. Ask the class if they think they can agree to use this Circle of Strength as a set of guidelines for their behaviors during their time in your program/school. Once everyone has agreed, have each person sign the Circle of Strength/Full Value Contract on their hand and post it in a place where it can be readily referenced for check-ins and debriefing and at any other time

Tip:

Remember these need not be exhaustive; you're going to be continuously checking in on your FVC/Circle of Strength.

Reflection:

1. How was it to come up with these behaviors and attitudes?

2. What do you notice about the words inside the Circle of Strength?

3. In what ways are these attitudes and qualities important to taking care of yourself and others?

4. How do put downs affect our ability to achieve our goals?

5. How can positive messages help us to achieve our personal and group behavioral goals?

6. What should we notice when things are going well in our class?

7. When things are not going well, how can the FVC help us?

Rules? What Rules?

Estimated Time

20 minutes

Description:

In this worksheet-driven activity, students deepen their commitment to their Full Value Contract.

Learning Themes:

- Demonstrate an understanding of each of the core Full Values.
- Describe the importance of rules and/or norms of behavior in a Full Value Community.
- Learn to express one's feelings verbally.

Props:

- 1 worksheet for each student
- The Circle of Strength you made in the activity on page 59

Setup:

Give each student a worksheet.

Framing:

"Today we are further creating our community by listing the details of our Full Value Contract/Circle of Strength. Use the worksheet to write down what each of the Values we have discussed means to you personally. Once you have finished, find another person who is done and begin to write down some specific things you can both agree to do (or not do) in order to be a part of this community. After all of our small teams are finished, we will share the ideas for each value."

Procedure:

1. Students write on the following worksheet their personal ideas for each Full Value.

2. Once students have completed their worksheets, they should share their ideas with another student.

3. These pairs present their ideas to the whole group

Reflection:

1. Now that we have thoughts about each value, look back on your personal worksheet; is there anything we need to add to our Circle of Strength?

2. Is there anything that we need to remove from the Circle of Strength?

3. How was it to express your ideas in the big group?

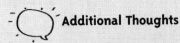

Additional Thoughts

• *Even though the reflection lists only three questions, it should be a directed, in-depth conversation about the Full Values and the behaviors that support them. You will want to explore each addition and subtraction with the whole group and make decisions about adding or subtracting.*

Contract Garden

Estimated Time

20 minutes

Tip:

The outcomes of Contract Garden, The Being and the Village are similar to the Circle of Strength. Each one has a different visual representation.

Description:

In this art activity, students will expand upon their Full Value Contract.

Learning Themes:

• Describe and demonstrate what it means to be a contributing member of a Full Value community.

• Describe the importance of rules and/or norms of behavior in a Full Value Community.

• Exhibit an ability to collaborate as part of a team including leading and following.

Props:

• Markers

• Flip chart or poster paper

• Any art materials you'd like

• The Circle of Strength you made in the activity on page 59

Setup:

Make sure your Circle of Strength is hung prominently on the wall in the room in which you are working.

Framing:

"You are entering your garden in the state fair. It will be judged by how well you integrate the Full Value Contract/our Circle of Strength. Think of things in a garden that represent items from our Full Value Contract/Circle of Strength. You (students) are creating a flower garden. You should show yourself as a flower. Add into your garden items that will help you grow. Also create ways to keep out anything that would hurt your garden. Name these on your drawing (i.e., bug spray keeps out the nasty comments about each other.)"

Procedure:

1. Give your students the art materials. (For a larger group, you may want to create a larger piece of paper by taping a couple of pieces of flip chart or poster paper together.)

2. Let them know that the idea is to expand the basic Full Value Contract by creating a visual representation of the individuals in the group plus what threatens and what supports the group.

3. Give them time to discuss what their garden should look like as well as time to draw.

4. Once drawn, have your students in the group sign their name to the addition to the Contract/Circle of Strength. This will help them to be aware of what their resources and challenges are.

Reflection:

1. Did we abide by our values as we were doing this activity?

2. What leaders emerged during this activity?

3. How will we be able to check our growth with our garden?

Variations

Let the group decide what kind of symbol fits their group's Full Value community. It doesn't have to be a garden! A flag, bus, space ship or the like is great too.

Tower of Power

Tip:

25 minutes

Description:

In this moderately active project, students construct a tower that represents their community.

Learning Themes:
- Manage one's behavior in accordance with the Full Value Contract.
- Describe the importance of rules and/or norms of behavior in a Full Value Community.
- Define and identify ways of caring for and helping self and others.

Props:
- 50-100 9-12 inch balloons
- Masking tape
- Markers

Setup:
Clear a relatively large space in your classroom.

Framing:
"Nourishing communities, the kinds that help you be your best, are founded upon strong friendships and respectful relationships. This activity explores what we need from others to build the kinds of connections that promote nourishing communities."

Procedure:
1. Separate your students into six equal (or as equal as possible) groups; representing each of the Full Values (Be Here, Be Safe, Be Honest, Set Goals, Care for Self and Others and Let Go and Move On).
2. Give each group several balloons and markers.
3. Have masking tape available.
4. Explain to the class that they are going to record the thoughts from Rules? What Rules? (activity found on page 61) on the balloons. Each group should focus on their assigned value using the thoughts from Rules? What Rules? as fodder, but they can expand as they see fit.
5. Tell each group to blow up the balloons, tie them off and write only one idea that captures their Full Value per balloon.

   They have five minutes to complete this part of the activity.

6. Have the class come together and share what is written on the balloons. Ask if anything is missing and then add balloons if needed. At this time, you should add anything that is missing on your Circle of Strength that your students have not put in – any norm that you feel needs to be there.

7. Explain to the class that the next challenge is to take all of the balloons using only masking tape as an additional prop, and build the tallest, free-standing tower possible.

8. Tell students that the finished structure represents the group's "Tower of Power" for building and maintaining positive relationships in their healthy learning community.

Reflection:

1. Did you demonstrate some of the qualities/behaviors you wrote on your balloons as you built the Tower of Power? What were the specific qualities you demonstrated?

2. For each student: Tell us about one thing you can do that will continue to improve your relationships with the people around you.

3. Are there any other behaviors we need to add to our Circle of Strength?

> **Tip:**
>
> *Add behaviors to your Circle of Strength as needed. If you've agreed to it, put it in writing!*

Variations

- *Limit one idea to each balloon but use as many balloons as there are ideas.*
- *You can keep the groups divided and have them each build a separate Tower of Power. Then bring the groups together to connect the six individual Towers into one for the entire class.*

Section IV:
Building Community Using Full Value

The theme of this section is to further build a nourishing, healthy community. Again, this community building through the use of a Full Value Contract really sets the stage for achieving the desired results of growth and change. By continued focus and development of values, your community can develop the skills necessary to manage their individual group behaviors more effectively.

This section focuses on activities that allow you to engage in the process of building community within your program or classroom.

Activities:

- Back Talk
- Carpet Ride
- Egg Protector
- Frantic
- Natural Disaster
- Paradigm Shift
- Yurt Circle

Back Talk

Description:

In this low-key activity, students explore the role of communication in the Full Values.

Learning Themes:

- Demonstrate an ability to appropriately express one's needs and emotions.
- Define and/or demonstrate the ability to compromise.
- Understand conflict and reactions to conflict.
- Know and appreciate one's peers.

Props:

- Play dough
- Colored straws
- Popsicle sticks
- Pipe cleaners
- Enough sculpting materials to make certain that each partnership has identical materials

Estimated Time

20 minutes

Setup:
Divide materials into identical piles, one for each person.

Framing:
"Have you ever explained something to someone and felt certain that they understood exactly what you meant only to discover later that they completely misunderstood your original intention? Being supportive involves the accurate transfer of thoughts and feelings, but sometimes that is difficult to achieve. Let's see how we do…"

Procedure:

1. Ask the students to each find a partner.
2. Divide the materials into identical groups for each pair.
3. Each partner receives identical materials. Have partners sit back to back.
4. Instruct the partnerships to create a sculpture that represents letting go and moving on.
5. Be very clear that each person in the partnership is creating the same sculpture as their partner simultaneously, coming up with an image of what letting go and moving on "looks like."

6. Partners must verbally describe their co-creations during the process but may not turn around or show one another what they are doing.

7. The goal is for each partnership to create identical sculptures without looking at each other's creations until both agree that the task is complete.

8. After both agree, partners should turn around and show their sculptures to one another.

Reflection:

1. Remember that the objective was for each partner to create an identical structure while sitting back to back. What surprised you most when you turned around?

2. How did you and your partner decide what to create? Where was the leadership?

3. How did you describe/communicate with each other?

4. What types of conflict and compromise occurred during this process?

5. How did you prevent conflict from occurring or manage conflict when it did occur?

6. What is one thing you appreciate about your partner?

Carpet Ride

Estimated Time

25 minutes

Tip:

This challenging activity can result in a level of frustration that you may have to help manage.

Description:

This activity requires students to work together in close physical proximity.

Learning Themes:

• Describe the skills needed to set healthy personal and/or group goals.

• Demonstrate an ability to evaluate and revise personal and/or group goals.

• Describe how one's choices and decisions impact the achievement of goals.

• Support each other in achieving goals and making decisions.

Props:

• Markers

• 1 piece of flip chart paper per three students

• Boundary markers (ropes, cones, etc.)

Setup:

Clear a space about 20 feet long. Define one end as the start. There should be enough width along the start and finish lines for your students to stand in groups of three side by side, while standing on their flip chart paper. Define the other end as the finish line.

Framing:

"Sometimes our goals are like magic carpets – they can take us to amazing places. These may be places we've dreamed of, but also may be places we've never dreamed of."

Procedure:

1. Separate your students into teams of three and give each group a piece of flip chart paper.

2. Have the students draw or write their behavioral or academic goals for the week on the paper.

3. The paper should be placed on the ground lengthwise with one end facing the start line and one end facing the finish line. (Doing this activity on carpeted or tiled floors works best.)

4. Students can opt to take their shoes off (the activity works better this way).

5. Explain that the object of the activity is for each group of three to cross the space in front of them using the flip chart paper as their magic carpet. Students need to take care of their resource (magic carpet)! Each time it tears or someone steps off, the small group has to stop and think about how they can work more efficiently before they can move forward.

6. Give students three minutes to plan a strategy for moving the paper before they start. They may not touch the paper while planning.

7. Have all teams begin at the same time. All members must be standing on the paper once the activity starts.

8. Activity is not over until all teams have crossed the finish line or the magic carpet is destroyed.

9. Keep the magic carpets.

Reflection:

1. How was it to cross this space using your goal team?

2. What goals did you write down for this activity?

3. If the paper represented your goal for the week, how did this activity affect how you think you will achieve your goal?

4. Can you name some ways that goals change within the time period we work on them?

5. What and/or who affects your goals?

6. How do your peers affect your goals?

 Tip:

You can either use the Reflection questions or use the Learning Log Reflection Activity.

Tip:

Use the Learning Log worksheet as a Reflection Activity whenever you'd like!

Reflection Activity Optional

LEARNING LOG

1. After an activity or at the end of a session/week, have each student fill out the Learning Log worksheet found in the Appendix of this book.

2. Provide students with the opportunity to share the thoughts they came up with using the Learning Log worksheet with their small and the entire group.

LEARNING LOG VARIATION:

• Compile and use as a long-range measurement of progress.

Variations

• *Have a variety of sizes of paper to choose from.*

• *Allow teams to form in a variety of numbers.*

• *Each student has their own magic carpet, but they still work as a team to traverse the area.*

Egg Protector

Description:

In this team initiative, students further explore goal setting.

Learning Themes:

- Learn to work together to achieve a common goal or task.
- Learn to express one's feelings verbally.
- Demonstrate an ability to evaluate and revise personal and/or group goals.
- Demonstrate social awareness through empathic and caring statements and/or behavior.

Props:

- 20 straws per group
- 36 inches of tape per group
- 1 egg per group
- Garbage bag, paper towels and a trash can for cleanup
- Flip chart paper
- Markers

Estimated Time

1 hour

Setup:

1. Open the garbage bag and tape it to the floor on the far side of the open space. (Your students will be dropping their protected eggs from six feet high onto this spread-out bag).

2. You can place a chair near or on the bag for students to stand on and drop their egg from, if this feels safe. If not, your students can simply drop their eggs from as high as they can reach when they are standing.

Framing:

"Life is challenging. Some of the things we experience can be very positive and help us grow and mature. Other experiences can be very hurtful. It is important that we learn to help support each other."

Procedure:

1. Separate the group into teams of four to six people.

2. Give each team an egg, 36 inches of tape, 20 straws, flip chart paper and markers.

3. Explain to the students that the challenge of this activity is to construct a container for their eggs that will prevent them from breaking when dropped from a height of six feet. The egg represents a student (no one in particular). The straw and tape of the container represents constructive feedback. The six-foot drop represents a giant put-down.

4. Tell students that the egg must be inside the container/network somehow (the straws cannot be used as a nest on the floor that the egg drops into) and should be able to withstand a drop from six feet.

5. Also explain that the second part of the challenge is to create a name and a commercial for their support container that lets everyone know why theirs is the best, most protective, most efficient support system known to human kind. They can make posters for their commercials and/or act them out for the whole group – whichever they choose.

6. Tell the teams that they have 20 to 30 minutes to develop their support container/network and commercial. Each team will present their commercial just before dropping their eggs.

7. After 20 to 30 minutes, gather everyone in a large group. Have students sit on the floor of the room in a horseshoe shape so that there is sort of a stage in the middle for the egg drops.

8. Ask for volunteers to start the presentation process and have the first team present their commercial and drop their egg. Each team should have a representative drop the team's egg from a height of about six feet or just have him/her reach up as high as he or she can and drop it from there.

9. Save the posters from the commercials to post.

Tip:

This is a great time to have the students join you in celebrating – even if the team you're celebrating breaks an egg!

Reflection:

1. What are some common themes in effective support networks?

2. What were you surprised by during this activity and why?

3. What feelings were you experiencing as you (or your team member) let go of the egg?

4. How can you transfer those same feelings of letting go with our community?

 Additional Thoughts

Occasionally an egg will break. Use this as an opportunity to discuss what happens when people can't accept constructive feedback or have challenges creating effective support networks.

Frantic

Description:
Frantic is a fast-paced activity in which students investigate success and failure.

Learning Themes:
- Describe how one's choices and decisions impact the achievement of goals.
- Support each other in achieving goals and making decisions.
- Know from whom and how to get assistance.

Props:
- Balloon or small beach ball for each student
- 10 extra balloons or small beach balls
- Boundary rope
- Markers

 Estimated Time

15 minutes

 Tip:

In every activity, be sure your students understand the directions and have the opportunity to ask for clarification.

Setup:
1. Clear a large open space in your classroom.
2. Divide the room in half with boundary rope.

Framing:
"We need to try to keep your goal (balloons) SMART. In this case, it means that you will launch your goal and try to make it land on the other side of the classroom, but you need help. As a team, you will try to not let others' goals (balloons) land on your side. The rules are: 1) you can only hit the balloon and 2) no catching or trapping the balloon. Once the balloon has touched the ground, leave it. Let's see which team can get most of the balloon (goals) on the other side?"

Procedure:
1. Pass one balloon or small beach ball to each person.
2. Ask students to blow up the balloons and tie them off.
3. Tell the students that the balloons represent their goals and ask them to write one of their goals on their balloons. You may want them to quickly establish a simple team symbol (i.e., a star or triangle) to write along with their goal to prevent confusion when keeping score.
4. Explain to your students that their challenge is to keep their goals SMART by getting them (the balloons) to the opposing team's side of the room.

5. Each balloon/goal in your opponent's area is one point for your team.

6. Make sure everyone understands your directions. Start on the count of three or whatever works for you.

7. Stop the activity when all the balloons are on the floor or in a few minutes. It will be more frantic if you manage the activity for a quick pace. Encourage students to use time between rounds to plan.

8. Play multiple rounds and add variations below as desired.

Reflection:

1. Can someone describe what happened when you tried to manage everyone on your teams' goals versus just your own?

2. What happened to your focus when balloons started touching the ground?

3. How do you think this kind of juggling or failure to juggle relates to being overwhelmed?

4. Name some ways in which we kept our goals alive.

5. How did we help each other to keep our goals?

6. How did you feel when/if you saw your goal land?

7. What are some examples of situations in your life when you would need help from caring adults in managing your goals?

 Additional Thoughts

You can substitute small beach balls for balloons.

Variations

• *Have your students label the extra balloons as detractors, things that get in the way of achieving goals (i.e., using drugs, losing their tempers, etc.). When the detractors land in your opponent's territory, you get three points.*

• *Add balloons in the second round to make it more challenging.*

Natural Disasters

Description:
In Natural Disasters, students experience the effects of helping or not helping one another.

Learning Themes:
- Analyze potential consequences when confronted with a behavior choice.
- Define and identify ways of caring for and helping self and others.
- Demonstrate self-awareness through the expression of thoughts and feelings.

Props:
One 10 to 24 inch rope per student or 1 Hula™ type hoop per student

Estimated Time

20 minutes

Setup:
None

Framing:
"Each of us is unique; we have our own place in the world. Spread your rope on the floor and stand inside it. Make sure your feet are all the way inside your loop (or hoop). Don't get too comfortable though; there is lots of flooding in this land and we have to work together to keep ourselves and each other safe."

Tip:

One solution is for students to sit on the floor with their feet within the rope.

Procedure:
1. Explain that people are safe only when they have both feet inside a loop and that the loops cannot be moved or re-tied into larger loops.
2. Before any movement takes place, do a quick check-in with the class, having each student take a moment to identify one of the things that keeps him or her safe.
3. Tell students that when they hear the words "Rain's coming," they must move to a new loop. Remind them that to be safe, they must have both of their feet within the perimeter of the loop.
4. Explain to students that they can take as much time as needed to find a new space and they can walk on the floor spaces between loops to get to a new place.
5. After two or three changes, acknowledge safe behaviors and increase the challenge by removing one or more of the loops. This will force someone to share his/her loop. Repeat this several times until many students are sharing loops with one another.
6. Keep removing loops.
7. The final goal is to include everyone inside one loop.

Reflection:

1. What were the initial challenges of this activity?

2. How did the challenge change as the activity progressed?

3. How did you take care of peers in your group?

4. Are your patterns in this activity the same as in the classroom (for example: me first, just save my friends, look for ways to help)?

5. What sacrifices did you make to save your peers?

6. What do you do in the classroom to help your peers?

 Additional Thoughts

• *You will need loops of different sizes with one loop that can fit all of the students' feet.*

• *Don't make it too easy as people can fit into a smaller loop than they think.*

Hint: They only have to have their feet in the loop.

Paradigm Shift

 Estimated Time

10 minutes

 Tip:

This is a great activity for students to lead with others including new group participants.

Description:

This is an individual activity. It is likely that students will have different individual experiences and "aha" moments. The focus is on perspective. This is a quick activity that you can use and re-use.

Learning Themes:

• Exhibit an ability to accept, acknowledge and appreciate differences.

• Identify the ways in which having differences on a team helps that team to accomplish its goals.

• Demonstrate social awareness through empathic and caring statements and/or behavior.

Props:

None

Setup:

None

Framing:

"The way we look at things defines how we think about ourselves and others. Being able to understand our own perspective and to consider new/different approaches is essential to supporting one another."

Tip:

This activity is much more complex than it sounds and can lead to great insights.

Procedure:

1. Ask your students to stand in a circle.
2. Ask them to imagine that there is an analog (an old fashioned round clock, not digital) clock on the ceiling, facing downward.
3. Have students each point one index finger toward their imaginary clock, fully extending that arm upward and circling it clockwise (they will be standing still, moving just one arm).
4. They should keep moving their arms clockwise pointing to where they see 12, then to 3, 6, 9 and back to 12.
5. Tell students to continually watch the tip of their finger and continue circling throughout the exercise.
6. Ask students to slowly lower their fingers by bending their elbows. Note that the finger remains pointing upward toward the clock and continues to circle.
7. Have them continue bending their elbows until their fingers are below their chins, then have them look down at their circling finger.
8. Ask students to observe in what direction the finger is now circling.
9. Have students repeat the process a couple of times on their own.

Reflection:

1. Most students will be a bit surprised to find that their finger is now going counterclockwise. Ask them, "How did this happen?"
2. Most students will say that it is from looking at things from a different point of view. "What do you think would happen if you looked at your problems from a different point of view?"
3. Can someone share an example of how they might support other students more effectively if they approached them from a different point of view?
4. How do you think this activity relates to the expression "Walk a mile in my shoes?" This is a great journaling question. Ask the group to journal for five minutes and then share their thoughts.

Additional Thoughts

Some students will turn their hand as they bring the finger downward, resulting in no change of direction. That's OK! Ask them to try again. And then explain that if you automatically adjust, by turning your hand, the direction of the circle won't change. You can choose to highlight this as an example of our natural tendency to keep things "status quo" and the challenge of changing perspectives.

Yurt Circle

Estimated Time

30 minutes

Description:

This activity requires students to physically rely on each other to maintain stability and balance.

Learning Themes:

- Define and demonstrate the ability to give and receive trust.
- Know from whom and how to get assistance.
- Define and identify ways of caring for and helping self and others.

Props:

None

Setup:

None

Framing:

"Today we are going to work more on developing our Care for Self and Others Value. This requires a little bit of trust on the part of your peers. We all have an expectation of trust and supporting each other within our community. If we are doing both of those things, we will be taking care of each other and ourselves."

Procedure:

1. The objective is for the whole group to support each other while leaning in whichever way designated.
2. Students start in a circle, holding hands.
3. Students should step back, while holding hands and remain in a circle, until everyone's arms are outstretched. Everyone should then count off as a "1" or a "2." All the 1s will lean in and all the 2s will lean out. Be sure they all start at the same time and lean slowly. Students should be able to lean without falling and while maintaining the circle. Sometimes groups are able to lean quite deeply.
4. After successfully completing their first lean, have everyone slowly stand up and reverse the direction in which they lean.

Reflection:

Reflection Activity:

1. Ask each 1 to pair up with a 2.

2. Have each pair discuss the following:

- Name three people you lean on to help you get your needs met.
- Identify whether or not there is a specific need you lean on each of those three people for and if so, why.
- Identify at least one person who leans on you.
- Identify one problem you have that you think others may have.
- Discuss whether or not you think you could be a resource for other people with that problem

3. Have students report to the group at least one problem each member of the pair (two problems per pair) could be a resource to others for.

 Additional Thoughts

• Your students should have good traction.

• Be sure everyone leans slowly.

• Have group hold a well-tied loop of rope instead of hands if there are touching or hand strength issues.

Chapter Two:
Learning to Assess
My Group and Self

In a good adventure program, students are constantly assessing themselves and their peers. As a result, they gain significant 'self and other' awareness skills. This self-assessment builds what Albert Bandura's (1986) social cognitive theory defines as self-reflective capabilities – one's ability to think about, define and evaluate one's behavior. This chapter is designed to give students the skills they need to do that. The two fundamental assessment strategies Project Adventure uses, particularly in BMTA, are: 1) Control to Empowerment and 2) GRAB. Both strategies are explored more extensively in Project Adventure's trainings.

This chapter will explore the following assessment models preceded by activities that promote a student's ability to be aware of and express his or her own emotions. Activities that teach students to give and receive feedback also set the stage for using these assessment models. The expressing emotions and giving and receiving feedback sections can also be enhanced by the empathy section of the Acquiring Leadership Skills chapter found on page 211.

Simpson's Control to Empowerment Model

In this self-assessment model students learn to, increasingly, control their own behaviors. The assessment aspects include:

- When am I ceding control of my own behavior to others?
- What triggers behavior I believe I can't control?
- How can I gain control?
- How can I help my peers be aware of and control their behavior?
- How can my peers help me be aware of and control my behavior?

Cindy Simpson, BMTA thought leader, developed this model. As the group becomes empowered, the leaders are able to back off and allow the group members to manage the process. Adult leaders must maintain ultimate authority, but as students step up and provide management, they are the ones who are doing the work. Staff are able to stand by and act as guides to the process – coaching, encouraging, teaching, and intervening when it is necessary – present and vigilant for safety, quality and control purposes.

Students use the following Control to Empowerment scale to assess how well they and their peers are doing at managing their own behaviors.

CONTROL BY LEADERS   **EMPOWERMENT OF STUDENTS**

| 1 | 2 | 3 | 4 | 5 | 6 | 7 | 8 | 9 | 10 |

GRAB Assessment

The GRAB assessment categories cover a spectrum of concerns as they relate to growth and change.[7]

GRAB as an assessment strategy is an acronym for:

Goals

Readiness

Affect

Behavior

Students use this framework to assess their own and their peers' progress as well as their preparedness for next steps and activities. Quite frequently, students assess progress on their goals. The focus of this assessment is to have your students look more deeply into what they need to do to meet their goals and be ready for the next goal, program challenge or initiative they may need to confront. Having students determine what will help them be "Ready" for the next activity provides information on what skills, knowledge or motivational factors will be helpful. Assessing one's "Affect" allows an exploration of feelings. Given that feelings can drive one's behaviors or affect one's readiness for an activity, it is important for students to be able to reflect and make the connection between how they are feeling and what they are ready to do. Alongside the assessment of one's feelings is the assessment of one's "Behaviors." By looking at one's own behaviors or the behavior of the group, an assessment can be made about the interplay of these areas and provide clarity regarding what a group or individual is prepared or capable of doing. Gathering this knowledge from the class and the individuals within it provides invaluable feedback for both the students and the teacher.

Finally, this chapter examines common thought distortions – patterns of thinking that can lead to self-destructive behaviors. Helping students to identify their thinking errors will enable them to develop strategies for better self management.

Because the Full Value Contract is so important to a good therapeutic program and given the fact that it can only be enhanced by the insights your students are gaining, we revisit it briefly at the conclusion of this chapter.

---

7. A section in *Exploring Islands of Healing* (section 3, pp. 63-140) is devoted to a discussion of how Project Adventure's extended assessment model of GRABBSS works.

Section I: Expressing Emotions

The theme of this section is becoming in tune with and appropriately expressing one's own emotions. While young people typically have many of these skills, this section is designed to reinforce and/or refresh these.

Middle school counselor Susan Carney says, in her online article *Helping Teens Express Feelings*: "Teens who are skilled in managing emotions have insight into their own experience, feel understood by others, and are empowered to find their own solutions. On the other hand, teens lacking in these skills often have little self-awareness, feel alone and helpless, and have few coping resources."8

Our considerable experience working with young people who have been labeled at-risk has affirmed this statement. The ability to appropriately express one's emotions is a building block to self-awareness. As staff, we can model this for our students as well.

Activities:
- All Aboard
- Balloon Trolleys
- Creating a Feelings Chart
- Feelings Memory Game
- Pictures of Me

---

8. http://youthdevelopment.suite101.com/article.cfm/helping_teens_express_feelings

All Aboard

Estimated Time

20 minutes

Description:

This problem-solving activity asks students to collaborate with the added stressor of being in one another's physical space.

Learning Themes:

- Demonstrate an ability to appropriately express one's needs and emotions.
- Increase one's emotional vocabulary.
- Define and identify ways of caring for and helping self and others.
- Demonstrate social awareness through empathic and caring statements and/or behavior.

Props:

- 3' x 3' All Aboard platforms or 3' x 3' area on the floor delineated by masking tape (1 platform/taped off square per 10-12 students depending on their size)
- Extra carpet square or spot markers as needed
- Colored dots – stickers, not spot markers
- I Am About Cards*

Setup:

1. Place the platforms or make your squares in the center of a large open space in your room. Be sure to leave at least five feet of space between each platform.
2. There should be one platform for 10-12 students. Place an extra polyspot per extra student around the perimeter of the platform or for a physically larger student group.
3. The area should be small enough to present a challenge for everyone to get on board, but large enough so that it is possible to get everyone on board.

Framing:

"We have made an agreement to build a safe learning environment. Our environment is represented by the platform and surrounding spots. Your task is to support one another in getting everyone safely on board into this environment we've built. Before you start, think of emotional reactions you may have in this activity where you will be working together in tight quarters?" Give your students a minute to think and ask them to share the emotions they are comfortable sharing.

• Available from Project Adventure

Procedure:

1. The object is simply to get your whole group on a platform at one time without touching the floor or ground.

2. In order to be counted as "on the platform," each person needs to have both feet off the ground or on a polyspot.

3. The group's challenge is to hold a balanced position for at least eight seconds, i.e., no one touches the ground for eight measured seconds.

4. Proper spotting (If you feel you can't spot this or any activity properly – don't do it!) must be monitored by you and any method that appears to be unsafe (stacking people on top of one another, etc.) should not be allowed.

Tip:

Instead of holding their position for eight seconds, you could ask them to hold it while they sang one verse of Row, Row Your Boat *or the like.*

Reflection:

Reflection Activity

1. Spread the I Am About Cards on the table or the floor.

2. Ask each student to pick two cards. One should reflect how they thought they were going to feel about doing the activity and the second should reflect how they actually felt.

3. When they are ready, go around the group and ask each student to show everyone the pictures they chose and the feelings they think they reflect.

4. Ask your students if anyone found a big difference between how they thought they would feel and how they actually did feel. If so, ask them if they wouldn't mind sharing the differences and why they thought they had them.

5. Ask your students if anyone had emotions they shared with the group before or during the activity. If so, ask them if expressing their emotions helped to manage them better.

Balloon Trolleys

Estimated Time

50 minutes

Description:

In this moderate activity, students experience how unexpressed emotions can interfere with relationships.

Learning Themes:

- Increase one's emotional vocabulary.
- Learn to express one's feelings verbally.
- Exhibit an ability to collaborate as part of a team including leading and following.
- Understand the emotions underlying conflict.

Props:

- Balloons – 1 per student
- Masking tape, activity ropes or boundary markers to make a curvy path
- Masking tape and markers to write on balloons

Setup:

Set up a curvy path throughout your space. Make the turns challenging but not too tight as students will have to pass through the path while connected to one another. You can outline this path with masking tape, activity ropes or boundary markers.

Framing:

"Do you ever have emotions about another person that you don't share with them? If so, do those emotions get in the way of your relationship with that person? Maybe you've expressed those emotions to the other person, but they still get in the way? Think of what those emotions may be, but don't share them with us yet."

Procedure:

1. Pass one balloon to each student and ask them to blow up the balloons and tie them off. Offer assistance if they are concerned with blowing up balloons.

2. Ask each student to label their balloon with an emotion they have had that has gotten in the way of a relationship. Remind them that they won't need to share the relationship or the incident, but they will need to share the emotion.

3. Ask students to form a line with group members (if your group is larger than 12-15, you may want to separate into small groups – more people means more challenge), standing front to back, like a trolley. Have each student place a balloon between his or her self and the person in front of them.

4. The person at the front of the line will simply hold his or her balloon out in front.

5. Explain that they can only use each other's pressure to support the balloons – no hands, arms or legs.

6. Explain that the challenge is to move the entire group through the path while staying connected to one another and not allowing any of the balloons to hit the floor.

7. Have students place their hands on the shoulders of the person in front of them.

8. If a balloon hits the floor, the group in question should stop, retrieve the balloon, and the student who was in the front of the line moves to the end, putting his or her balloon between him or herself and the person in front of them. The group can then carry on from where they lost the balloon.

9. Have all your students form one large circle after each small group has finished the course.

Tip:

If you have the time and you feel your students would be responsive, you could explore the symbolism of not being able to use your hands or feet to hold up the balloon – how an unexpressed emotion really limits a relationship.

Reflection:

Reflection Activity:

1. Ask each student to share the emotion they wrote on their balloons.

2. Ask them why they think it got in the way. Remind them that they don't have to share the specifics. For example: "I wrote down Anger because being angry caused me to be mean." is perfect.

3. Finally, ask them if expressing their emotions would have prevented them from getting in the way of their relationship.

4. Let them express their emotions by popping their balloons with their partners. They should do this back-to-back, but they can use their hands and feet.

Additional Thoughts

• *Keep an eye out for emotional responses and comments regarding appropriate touching.*

• *Divide group into smaller groups if you are concerned with the students' abilities to manage physical closeness. You can also place the balloons between the students as they stand side by side, if that is more manageable. Also, offer the option for students to be spotters if they are uncomfortable with the given body positions.*

Creating a Feelings Chart

Estimated Time

20 minutes

Description:

In this low-key activity, students identify words to express their emotions.

Learning Themes:

- Increase one's emotional vocabulary.
- Learn to express one's feelings verbally.

Props:

- Markers or pens
- At least 20 index/note cards
- A piece of flip chart paper or two with each letter of the alphabet labeling an area
- Tape
- Optional – a list of the questions provided in the procedure that follows

Setup:

Prepare a piece of flip chart paper or two by labeling different areas of the paper with each letter of the alphabet. Your students will be taping index cards with a feelings word on them under the corresponding first letter to alphabetize the words.

Framing:

"It can be hard to tell people what you are feeling. Sometimes we just don't have the words. Together we are going to start a chart to help us find the right words."

Tip:

There is no right or wrong, just how your students feel. However, certainly challenge inappropriate or anti-social responses.

Procedure:

1. Ask your students to brainstorm words that describe feelings.
2. Ask for a volunteer to write each word on an index/note card.
3. When they have at least 10 words, ask them to tape each index/note card under the appropriate letter on the flip chart paper so they alphabetize the words.
4. Expand the chart by reading the following sentences for the students to finish. New words should be written on an index/note card.
   - When I make a mistake, I feel _____.
   - When I do a good job, I feel _____ .
   - When I help someone and they say, "Thanks," I feel _____.
   - When someone calls me a name, I feel _____ .

- When my friend gets a brand new IPod and I don't have one, I feel _____ .
- When someone won't share with me, I feel _____ .
- When I help someone else, I feel _____ .
- When someone smiles at me, I feel _____ .

5. Again ask your students to alphabetize these words.

Reflection:

Reflection Activity:

1. Separate your students into three equal or roughly equal groups.

2. Give each small group one or more starting letter for which your students currently have no words.

3. Challenge each group to come up with three or more new words using one or more of their starting letters. Let them know that they need to be words that describe a feeling and that they need to be prepared to define this word and use it in a sentence.

4. As groups report out, they should post new words on the flip chart paper.

5. Hang the Feelings Chart prominently. Add to it throughout the program. Encourage students to use the Chart to find words to express their emotions.

Variations

- *You could turn up the competition in the reflection activity by giving new words that start with a certain letter a point value. So, an A word might have three points and a Z word might have ten. The challenge for each group will then be to get the most points.*

- *Turn the reflection activity into a challenge for the whole group by asking them to come up with feelings words for each letter of the alphabet.*

Feelings Memory Game

Estimated Time

20 minutes

Tip:

You could create the cards with new words to expand students' vocabulary or use words generated in the Feelings Chart activity to reinforce students' vocabulary.

Description:

This low-key activity works to increase students' emotional vocabulary.

Learning Themes:
- Increase one's emotional vocabulary.
- Learn the subtle cues that people use to express their emotions.
- Demonstrate an ability to appropriately express one's needs and emotions.

Props:
- 24 index/note cards that have twelve pairs of feelings words written on them (12 words written twice – one word per card)

Setup:
1. Turn the cards face down on a table that is accessible on all sides.
2. Lay down a rope that will separate your students from the table with the cards.
3. Gather your students in a group on the side of the rope without the table.

Framing:

"This is an opportunity to explore feelings. Laid out before you are 24 face-down cards that have some, but certainly not all, feelings written on them. Your job as a group is to find matching pairs; each word has an identical partner. This is a timed activity. Take a moment or two to plan."

Procedure:
1. Explain the rules to your students. They are:
   - Students cross the line to the table and turn over two cards.
   - If the words are a match, the students should leave the cards face up.
   - If the words do not match, the students should turn the cards back over.
   - All cards must remain on the table.
   - The round is over when all cards have been matched – all cards have been turned over.
   - Time starts when a participant crosses the line.
   - The game starts when you say, "Go!"

1. Say "Go!" and start the game. Begin timing students when they cross the line.

2. Tell the group their time.

3. If there is time, have a second round with the group setting a goal regarding how fast they can accomplish the task before hand. Remember to shuffle the cards.

Reflection:

Reflection Activity

1. Separate your students into two small groups.

2. Give each group a set of the feelings cards. Each group should have one card of each of the pairs you made.

3. Ask the small groups to come up with a facial expression that expresses each feelings word. No words or non-facial expressions (i.e., foot stomping) allowed! Ask them to do this in such a way that the other group can't see or hear their work.

4. Give your students five minutes or so to do this.

5. Bring your students together in a large group.

6. Ask one small group to show one facial expression to the other small group and the other small group guesses the feeling it is expressing. When the feeling is guessed, switch group roles; one group expresses while the other guesses.

7. Play until feelings or your time runs out.

Pictures of Me

Estimated Time

60 minutes

Tip:

You can extend, divide or shorten this activity based on student interest.

Description:
This creative activity helps students become aware of their own emotions.

Learning Themes:
- Demonstrate self-awareness through the expression of thoughts and feelings.
- Describe the skills needed to set healthy personal and/or group goals.
- Describe a positive future for one's self.

Props:
- Paper (as large as possible – poster size is good, one sheet for each student)
- Materials for drawing, painting or creating collages
- If possible, frames for final products

Setup:
None

Framing:
"This activity is a great way to develop an appreciation for your own and your friends' emotions. In it, you will think about how you handled your emotions when you were a child, now and how you'd like to handle them going forward. In this activity, we are going to explore your handling of emotions through creative imagery. If you choose, you can draw an actual portrait of yourself, write a description of yourself or use images from magazines, nature, etc. The first picture of you will be…"

Procedure:
1. Give students one sheet of paper each and supplies to share and two additional sheets of white paper for the written bridge responses (see #5 and #7).
2. Ask students to fold the paper into three sections with the longest edge on the top and then open the paper so that there are three panels to work on.
3. Explain to students that they are going to be creating separate representations in each panel. In the first panel, have students create a representation of how they remember themselves handling their emotions as children. The description can be written, drawn, a collage, etc. or a combination of these.
4. In the middle panel, have students describe how they handle their emotions now.

5. Between the first and second panels they will create a bridge or connection by citing three messages received from others that influenced how they handle their emotions now (e.g., My father told me it is OK for boys to cry), and three messages students gave themselves that shaped how they handle their emotions now (e.g., I don't like to hold my anger in). The bridge will consist of six messages total.

6. Finally, in the third panel, ask students to illustrate how they would like to handle their emotions in the future.

7. Have students create another bridge or connection between the second and third panels stating three changes students can make that will help them achieve the emotion expression they desire (e.g., I can vent to my friends when I am angry at my teacher), and three messages students would like to give themselves as they progress toward their vision (e.g., it is normal to be angry at people even if you love them). Again, the bridge should consist of six messages total.

Reflection:
Reflection Activity:
Ask students to pair up with the person to their right. (A three-member group is fine to accommodate groups with an odd number of students.) In their small groups, they should share the stories of their pictures.

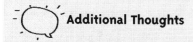 **Additional Thoughts**

This activity may be debriefed in a variety of ways. Students can share their images with the class after each panel is finished, or after the first and second panels are completed, then after the third is completed.

Section II: Giving and Receiving Feedback

This section's theme focuses on giving and receiving feedback so students can share their assessments of other students in a way that can be heard, understood and acted upon. The following activities will also help students receive feedback without becoming defensive or hurt.

The ability to receive feedback is essential to self-awareness and the mastery of social emotional skills. Good feedback can be seen as a gift to help one develop. The Project Adventure assessment model, Simpson's Control to Empowerment, is built upon the ability of the students as well as staff, to be good givers and receivers of feedback. Essentially, the ability of students to help one another grow is dependent on their ability to give and receive feedback. Assessments of students who are higher on the Control to Empowerment scale reveal a greater mastery of giving and receiving feedback. Teachers who take time to work on skill development in this area will help their students master all the social and emotional skill competencies necessary for an empowered environment.

Ideally, feedback is given in the spirit of caring and wanting to help your peer or student be a better person. Conversely, when a student receives feedback, it is (again ideally – this is hard for all of us) to be accepted as a gift to help one improve. One guideline for presenting feedback is that it should be: concise, concrete, caring and constructive. Consider using this guideline when presenting the concept of giving feedback to your students.

The activities in this section are fine tuned to the feedback skills, but you will find that your students are practicing the skills of giving and receiving feedback in the majority of the activities in this guide.

Activities:
- Bean Bag Tag
- Chaotic Team Juggle
- Don't Touch Me
- Frogger
- Name Roulette
- Strength Bombardment

Bean Bag Tag

Description:

In this activity, your students will be very active while exploring how being self-aware and discussing it enables them to be more productive.

Learning Themes:

- Understand how negative internal dialogue hinders relationship building.
- Demonstrate physical self-awareness.
- Listen to the feedback of one's peers.

Props:

- One bean bag for each student (they should be close to equal in size)

 Estimated Time

20 minutes

Setup:

1. Set boundaries (whatever works for your space, but make sure students have enough room to play tag at whatever pace works for the group and meets your goals for this activity)

2. Each person gets one bean bag to put on top of his or her head.

Framing:

"Has anyone ever heard the expression 'she has a real chip on her shoulder'? What does that mean?" Give students a few minutes to discuss, "Today we are going to play tag with a bean bag on our head."

Procedure:

1. Give each student a bean bag.

2. Explain that bean bags can only be touched when they are being placed on their heads.

3. Tell them or ask them to help you decide what the pace will be (i.e., fast walk, jog, etc.)

4. Explain that when you say, "Go!", everyone is going to begin playing a tag game with bean bags on their heads, even the person who is It.

5. Determine who your first It will be. Ask for volunteers or whatever works for you.

6. Explain that if anyone loses or touches their bean bag, they take a knee and simultaneously say, "Chip on my shoulder, bean bag on my head." They can then put the bean bag back on their head and continue.

 Tip:

You could make the metaphor more obvious by asking them to label their bean bag, using masking tape and a marker, with an attitude that they believe gets in the way of good relationships with others.

7. Ask them to put their bean bags on their heads.

8. Ask them to start with their hands out in "tagging position" to encourage them to keep their hands away from the bean bag.

9. Say "Go!" and start the play.

10. Play until time runs out or your students lose interest.

Reflection:

Questions for Discussion:

1. Was it hard to play tag with a bean bag on your head?

2. How is it to go through life with a 'chip on your shoulder'?

3. How is it to accept feedback if you have a 'chip on your shoulder'?

4. What can make it easier for you to accept feedback?

....

Chaotic Team Juggle

Estimated Time

40 minutes

Tip:

Don't worry – the labeling will make sense when you read through the activity!

Description:

This fast-paced activity is a variation of the traditional Group Juggle. Students practice giving feedback.

Learning Themes:

• Demonstrate physical self-awareness.

• Demonstrate an ability to appropriately express one's needs and emotions.

• Demonstrate and practice the ability to give and receive healthy feedback.

Props:

• Tossables

• Masking tape

• Markers

• Flip chart paper

Setup:

1. Separate your students into two groups. If your group is eight or fewer, don't split them.

2. Give each group a roll of tape and a few markers.

3. Keep the tossables until you have finished framing the activity and giving directions.

4. Label two tossables, more if your entire group numbers more than 15 with behaviors that would generate feedback (see step 8 for description).

5. Keep an unlabelled tossable or two, tape and markers ready in case you see a behavior during the activity that you'd like to add. (see the tip box)

Framing:

"If you think about it, people do a lot of juggling when they're in a community. On the one hand, there are behaviors that really drive you crazy. On the other hand, there are behaviors that make you feel: happy, proud, joyful, content and more. It is important to be able to tell people about the behaviors you think they need to improve on as well as all the good they do. This activity will help us explore how to do that."

Procedure:

1. Divide the group into two small groups, as evenly as possible.

2. Each member of Group One writes one statement on a piece of tape that describes a behavior that makes them want to give feedback. This statement should be about something in their "Opportunities for Growth" (i.e., what they need to work on).

3. Each member of Group Two writes one word or phrase on a piece of tape that would describe a strength that a person has.

4. Give each student a tossable and ask them to put their piece of tape on it.

3. With tossables in hand, have students gather into one large group. Then divide into two new groups. Each new group is roughly half Group One participants (Causes of Feedback – Opportunities for Growth) and roughly half of Group Two (Causes of Feedback – Strengths)

4. Starting with one tossable per group, have each group develop a throwing pattern using these guidelines:

   • You cannot throw to someone on your immediate right or left.

   • Each of you can only throw and catch one time while developing your pattern.

   • Once everyone has thrown once and caught the ball once, make sure that the pattern can be recreated.

   • Practice the pattern a number of times.

5. You may ask the group to set a goal regarding how many tossables they think they can juggle at once.

6. Students will now attempt to juggle as many of these "feedback prompters" as possible without dropping any. Start each group with just a few tossables, and gradually add more.

7. An amazing performance would be for a group to juggle one more tossable than there are people in the group!

8. Have some of the balls labeled in advance. Have one for each group doing the activity. Label these balls with words that reflect negative behaviors such as: Swearing, Name Calling, Not Sharing, etc. These should be real behaviors that students might exhibit and could elicit feedback from their peers.

9. Have each group practice using the balls that they labeled. Once each group has practiced juggling, create "chaos" by asking them to pass one of the balls you labeled around their circle clockwise or counter clockwise. Remind them to keep juggling the other balls in the former pattern that they had set up and practiced.

Tip:

If possible, mark the labels with behaviors that would evoke feedback about what to work on and is applicable to your group. For example, if it is a substance abuse group, label a ball 'Hanging out with kids who get high' or the like. Another great way to make it applicable is to use behavior you've observed in this activity – quickly label a tossable and, if needed, substitute it for one you've already made. 'Yelling' or 'Withdrawing' are some examples.

Reflection:

Reflection Activity

1. Have your students stay in their small groups and hold onto the tossables they now have.

2. If a student is holding a ball labeled with a Strength, how will he or she use it to give caring feedback? If students possess Negative or Opportunity for Growth labels, how will they frame their feedback so that it is caring and helpful?

3. Let them know that they are going to report this out to the whole group. Provide them with pens and paper to write their responses. Posting these responses will help them transfer their learning and experience.

4. Bring them back to the large group. Have one person from one group role play giving their decided-upon feedback to a student from the other group. Each pair should exchange two pieces of feedback, one from each student. After each exchange, have the whole group reflect on whether or not it was good feedback. If it was, what made it good? Some examples might be: it used 'I' statements; the giver made good eye contact; it valued some of the receiver's skills. If it wasn't good, what made it that way? Some examples might be: it was not specific; the giver raised his or her voice; the feedback did not tell the receiver how they could improve.

5. Write examples of good feedback on one piece of flip chart paper and examples of bad feedback on another. Post these for future reference.

Don't Touch Me

Estimated Time

20 minutes

Description:

In this team-oriented, problem-solving activity, students will begin to practice their feedback skills.

Learning Themes:

- Learn to work together to achieve a common goal or task.
- Understand and practice what it means to focus on another.
- Demonstrate and practice the ability to give and receive healthy feedback.

Props:

- 1 cone or poly dot per team
- 1 Hula Hoop®
- 1 slip of paper per person. On each slip, write a behavior or affect that the student will act out during this activity. Some examples are: happy person, grumpy person, quiet person, assertive person, questioning person etc. There should be no repeats per team.

Setup:

Creatively separate the class into two even groups. Place the hula hoop on the ground. Place the cones opposite one another. Each team lines up single file behind their cone. Once they are in teams, give individuals the behavior/affect slips of paper. Ask students to behave and act in the manner that the slip of paper describes, especially when they are interacting with the other groups.

Framing:

"Today we are going to practice our ability to give feedback to each other. As we have discussed before, feedback begins with observation so really turn up your observation skills and let's see what happens in this activity.

Procedure:

1. The goal is to have the groups change sides as quickly as possible, following the guidelines.
2. Play happens in two groups, each taking a side.
3. Say "Go" and start the timer.
4. While changing sides, each group must put some body part inside of the hoop.

5. There can be no physical contact with anyone else during the activity.

6. Any rule infraction will result in a three-second penalty added to the team's final time.

7. When more than one person is in a hoop, these players simultaneously yell, "Don't touch me." All players remember to keep their bumpers up.

8. All players will use their slips of papers to guide their affects and behaviors during the activity.

Reflections:

Ask students to gather with partners within their own team. Give each partnership the name of a person from the opposite team. Give the partnerships a piece of paper. Ask them to write something positive that they observed that person do and something constructive that they may need to change. The partners then give the person their feedback.

Comments & Variations

- *A suggested group size is 8-10 per team. With more people, separate into four teams, and have four cones. Play takes place across the square, everyone still having to go through the hula hoop.*

- *This version allows students to play out various roles and receive feedback for their behaviors. This is a less threatening start for giving and receiving feedback.*

- *If you are using the group process once the students have received and read their feedback, call a check-in group to see if there were any surprises, etc.*

Ahhhh Grasshopper aka Frogger

Description:

An active, engaging, playful activity that requires students to consider feelings while making physical gains with others tossing out distractions along the way

Learning Themes:

- Learn to work together to achieve a common goal or task.
- Demonstrate and practice the ability to give and receive healthy feedback.
- Manage one's behavior in accordance with the Full Value Contract.

Props:

- 1 Fleece ball per person
- Boundary markers
- Feelings spectrum work sheets
- Fill in the blank feedback worksheet (found in Appendix)
- Masking tape
- Markers
- A stop watch
- 1 polyspot per half group

Estimated Time

30 minutes

Setup:

Set up boundaries that are about the size of a basketball court, making it clear where the sides, ends and beginning are. Separate the group into two even groups. Hand out the spot markers to one of the small groups, give them the feelings spectrum hand-out and ask them to select one feeling from the top line, i.e., mad, sad, glad, afraid, confused etc. Each team member then writes down one feeling from that column on their polyspot. The group with the spot marker who are now considered the hoppers proceed down the length of the play area on the polyspots. The other group is trying to throw balls (distracters or escalators) at the polyspot hoppers.

Framing:

"Everyday we all experience a myriad of emotions. Sometimes we are able to manage those feelings and sometimes we choose to act out with our behaviors because we don't know what to do with our feelings. As we play this activity, try to have the feeling that is on your polyspot in your body and mind. I wonder how we can become accomplished at managing our feelings in this boggy environment where things are constantly being thrown at us?"

Procedure:

1. Polyspot hoppers are trying to get across the feelings bog (the boundary area). The goal is to get every hopper across the pond safely and quickly.

2. Hoppers are safe when they are on the polyspots or when they have arrived at the other end of the bog.

3. The distracters can slow down the progress of the hoppers by throwing fleece balls at them.

4. Distracters must stay out of the bog, i.e., behind the boundaries. They can only go into the bog to retrieve the fleece balls.

5. When a hopper is hit while not on a polyspot, he or she must go back to the beginning of the bog.

6. Hoppers move across the bog by hopping (with both feet) from one polyspot to another. Polyspots need to be tossed at least three feet forward.

7. A hopper gets off a feeling spot in order to toss it forward.

8. A hopper who makes it all the way to the other end becomes accomplished at managing feelings and becomes the Master Grasshopper which renders him or her immune to the distracting and escalating fleece balls. Those Masters are able to return to the bog and help other hoppers.

9. Time begins when the hoppers leave the start line and ends when all arrive at the end of the bog.

10. After the first round, have the groups switch roles.

Reflections:

- How did you do with this timed activity when there were all those distracting and escalating situations being thrown at you?

- Was your group successful?

- Give each student the blank feedback sheet. Assign students a partner and ask them to complete the feedback sheet for each other. When the group is complete have the students hand each other the written feedback and read what their peers observed.

Comments & Variations

The written feedback sheet could be a complete lesson in itself.

Name Roulette

Description:

In this low-key activity, students demonstrate appreciation for one another's strengths.

Learning Themes:

- Demonstrate and practice the ability to give and receive healthy feedback.
- Evaluate and observe the behaviors, attributes and strengths of others.

Props:

- A Hula™ type hoop
- Clay and/or other sculpture making materials

Estimated Time

30 minutes

Setup:

None

Framing:

"Each of us has special abilities and traits. These go well beyond what we look like. These strengths make us individual and unique. It is important that we identify and use our strengths as we learn and grow. It is also important that we tell one another about our strengths and give each other positive feedback, so that we feel appreciated and keep doing those things that are working."

Procedure:

1. Separate students into two groups and ask each group to make a circle with everyone facing the center.

2. Put the two circles together so that it looks like the number eight.

3. Place the hoop where the two circles meet, flat on the floor so that one person from each circle is standing in it.

4. Tell students that when you say "Go!", the two circles will begin to rotate in opposite directions, either clockwise or counterclockwise. Decide on the direction before you say "Go!".

5. Let them know that when you say "Stop!", two people (one in each circle) will be standing back to back in the hoop and that when you say "Look!", those two people should spin around and the first of the pair to name the other person wins that person for their circle.

6. After several rounds, let your students know that you are going to change the challenge a bit. This time when you say "Stop!", each group needs to posi-

Tip:

The suggested sculpture is more about giving your students an opportunity to express themselves non-verbally than a sculpture specifically. So, feel free to substitute music, dance or another reflection activity!

tively describe the other group's part of the pair (person with their back to your group) without using any physical characteristics. For example, if Katie and Lisa are back to back, Katie's circle will describe Lisa to Katie without using any physical attributes until Katie says the name Lisa or vice versa. You can't say blonde hair, but you could say good listener.

7. The first person in the pair to say the other person's name wins that person for their circle.

Reflection:

Reflection Activity:

1. Give each student a lump of clay and/or other sculpture making materials.

2. Ask them to make a sculpture that reflects how they felt when their peers were saying nice things about them. Remind them 1) that this is simply a way to express how they feel, not something that is being judged for its beauty and 2) that they will need to show and talk about their sculptures to the group.

3. Give them ten or so minutes to complete their sculptures.

4. Bring them back together and have them show and talk about their sculptures.

Follow up with these questions for discussion:

1. Tell me what it was like to try to describe each other without using physical characteristics.

2. Were you surprised at how many traits we share?

3. How do you think our strengths will help us to continue to establish a safe learning community?"

4. Why do you think it is important to tell each other about our strengths?

Strength Bombardment

Description:

In this thoughtful activity, students will use their observation skills to give feedback to each other.

Learning Themes:

- Listen to the feedback of one's peers.
- Give and receive feedback that is in line with the Full Value Contract.
- Manage behavior while receiving feedback.
- Evaluate and observe the behaviors, attributes and strengths of others.

Props:

- A watch to measure 30 seconds

Estimated Time

20 – 30 minutes

Setup:

Arrange the class so that they are seated in a circle and everyone can see one another. You will need the watch.

Framing:

"Here is an opportunity for everyone to feel really good about themselves by the time we are done today. It is up to each of you to make this happen for each other. It involves being thoughtful listeners and speakers.

Procedure:

1. Have the class gather in a seated circle.
2. Each person will have the opportunity to receive feedback from everyone in the class.
3. Each student will have 30 seconds to listen to all their peers bombard them with these strengths and attributes.
4. The group can all speak at the same time – no shouting.
5. The feedback is to be about the qualities they have observed in each other, i.e., "You show good leadership. You have a quiet voice but good things to say." Stay away from physical attributes or possessions, i.e., "I like your hair. I admire all the music on your ipod."
6. Pause for a moment before starting with the next student so that everyone has time to think.
7. Stick to 30 seconds?

Reflections:

1. Ask the group to find their journals and write a list of all the things that they heard about themselves today.

2. What surprises did they have?

3. Is there anything they may do differently having heard today's information from their learning community?

4. Think about your behavioral goal this week. Did any of the information you received impact how you might think about or change that goal?

Section III: Control to Empowerment

The theme of this section is learning Simpson's Control to Empowerment Scale as a tool for self assessment. The desired outcome is to help students gain more in control of their behavior as they become more self aware.

Activities:

- Blind Polygon
- Bridge It
- Left Right Pairs Tag
- Let's Win
- Pi Chart the word *behavior*
- Quality Control
- Where RU on the Scale?

Blind Polygon

Description:

In this activity, students explore how they make decisions and how decisions affect outcomes.

Learning Themes:

- Solve problems by analyzing causes and potential solutions.
- Analyze potential consequences when confronted with a behavior choice.
- Display an ability to make decisions that support community norms and pro-social behaviors.
- Exhibit an ability to collaborate as part of a team including leading and following.

Props:

- 1 60' length of rope
- Flip chart paper (7 sheets)
- Markers

Estimated Time

35 minutes

Setup:

1. Clear a large, open space.
2. Tie the ends of the rope together in a square knot – to form a large circle.

Tip:

This activity is framed around decision making which is a skill you are trying to develop. The reflection is around Control to Empowerment. Don't be afraid to let an activity do double duty when it fits!

Tip:

Make it more challenging with harder shapes – a pentagon, a star, etc.

Tip:

Does what your students think happened coincide with what you saw? For example, is Joe saying he made active decisions when you saw him get pulled around? If so, check in with the group.

Tip:

You could really play up the idea of being led blindly when you are passive in this activity.

Framing:

"Let's start to explore decision making. You will simply close your eyes in this problem-solving activity. So, you won't have all the information. See if you actively or passively problem solve."

Procedure:

1. Ask your students to stand in a fairly open circle around the rope.

2. Lay the rope on the ground at their feet.

3. Explain to them that the object of the activity will be to work as a group to form the rope into different shapes while everyone who will be holding the rope has their eyes closed.

4. Tell the students that they must be holding the rope and can talk with one another throughout the process, but the real challenge will be to keep their eyes closed.

5. After checking for questions, ask the group to close their eyes, reach down and grab the rope, stand up and form a square.

6. Tell your students to let you know when they feel as though they have made a square, at which time they can open their eyes and see what shape they are in!

7. Consider repeating the process having the students make a triangle and a circle.

Reflection:

1. How many people made mostly active decisions?

2. Can you describe those for us and why you think they were active?

3. How many people made mostly passive decisions?

4. Can you describe those for us and why you think they were passive?

5. Do you think you would have solved the problem if you were all passive decision makers?

6. Do you think you would have solved the problem if you were all active decision makers? You might follow with: Would it have been slower to solve the problem if everyone was trying to make an active decision at the same time?

Reflection Activity:

1. Separate your students into groups of three or four. Have each group brainstorm about when they felt controlled and when they felt empowered during this activity. They should also brainstorm why they felt this way.

2. Have each small group report out their thoughts.

Bridge It

Estimated Time

45 minutes

Description:

In this moderately active initiative, students explore the role of communication in empowerment.

Learning Themes:

- Define and/or demonstrate the ability to compromise.
- Solve problems by analyzing causes and potential solutions.
- Display an ability to make decisions that support community norms and pro-social behaviors.
- Exhibit an ability to collaborate as part of a team including leading and following.

Props:

- 16 balls
- 16 plastic cups
- 16 pieces of paper
- 16 straws
- 8 balloons
- 4 rolls of tape
- 4 index cards with "new language" on each

Setup:

1. Create four separate spaces within your area. Try to find or create spaces in which students from other groups will not see one another.

2. Place four balls, four plastic cups, four straws, four pieces of paper, two balloons and a roll of tape in each space.

3. Each group also gets a card with their "language" on it. (See sample language cards at the end of this activity.) The challenge is for the group to use the language on the card when communicating with other groups. They can use common language when in their smaller group.

Framing:

"Sometimes we are in control. Sometimes we need to rely on other people to be in control so that we stay safe, or honest, or see the situation from a different perspective. Let's experience what it is like to rely on others to see the big picture."

Procedure:

1. Ask the students to divide themselves into four equal groups and move to one of the four spaces.

2. Explain that the objective is for each small group to build a bridge that looks as much like the other bridges as possible and that is able to connect with the other bridges.

3. The sequence begins with a five-minute meeting with a chosen representative from each small group. Refer to communication rules below.

   Communication Rules:
   - A new representative from each small group should be chosen each time a negotiating session is held.
   - The groups work independently of each other, but are allowed three planning/negotiating meetings together as an entire group.
   - During the planning/negotiation sessions, only one spokesperson from each small group can talk.
   - Communication among groups is guided by the language cards (each small group has a separate language card).

4. There is a seven-minute discussion and building back at the site in their small group.

5. Another five-minute planning/negotiating session (new representatives from each group) is held.

6. This is followed by a five-minute discussion and building time back at site in the small group.

7. Another five-minute planning/negotiating session (new representatives from each group) is held.

8. Then a five-minute building time in the small group.

9. Finally, the "unveiling" takes place with each small group bringing their bridge to the center of the room to see how the bridges match and compare. You can also have students rotate through each construction site and come together in one large group for the reflection.

Reflection:

1. What was it like to try to communicate with the other groups?

2. What were the differences between what it was like in the large group meetings versus the small group meetings?

3. Were there times you gave up control and empowered others to take control or be in charge?

4. Were you more in control in one role than the other?

5. How did trying to control what your small group did feel?

6. Do you think it is easier to control yourself or control others?

7. How do you think this experience relates to control to empowerment?

 Tip:

Basically the language cards use words that are relevant to the topic, but make no sense in terms of connections to the actual objects. So, feel free to make cards you think fit best.

Sample Language Cards:

GROUP 1	GROUP 2	GROUP 3	GROUP 4
Ball = Manage	Ball = Behave	Ball = Value	Ball = Appropriate
Cup = Respect	Cup = Caring	Cup = Team	Cup = Goal
Paper = Concise	Paper = Control	Paper = Thnik	Paper = Friend
Straw = Empower	Straw = Self	Straw = Teacher	Straw = Responsible
Balloon = Others	Balloon = Assess	Balloon = Happy	Balloon = Overpowered
Tape = Act Out	Tape = Kindness	Tape = Irresponsible	Tape = Thoughtful

Left Right Pairs Tag

Estimated Time

10 minutes

Tip:

This activity takes a small, but important step in helping students realize that they are making decisions all the time.

Description:

In this quick activity, students reflect on the role of goal-setting in empowerment.

Learning Themes:

- Exhibit an ability to collaborate as part of a team including leading and following.
- Analyze potential consequences of following others.
- Display an ability to make decisions that support community norms and pro-social behaviors.

Props:

- 4 cones

Setup:

Set out four cones to mark the boundaries for a tag game.

Framing:

"Awareness and understanding of personal goals help people make decisions – take action – in a way that is consistent with what they feel is important. It is one way in which people become empowered. This activity will help you to experience achieving a goal and provide insight into what motivated or influenced your ability to do that."

Procedure:

1. Ask each student to find a partner and stand side by side.
2. Tell the students that they are going to play a fun tag game with their partners.
3. Ask the people standing on the left-hand side of the partnership to raise their hands to identify themselves. These people can only move straight forward or to the left with a 90-degree angle turn. Model this motion.
4. Ask the people standing on the right-hand side of the partnership to raise their right hands to identify themselves. Explain that these people can only move straight ahead or to the right with a 90-degree angle turn. Model this motion.
5. Explain that the turns need to be square, right angles, not arcs. Model what not to do with the arcs and then reaffirm acceptable 90-degree turns.

6. Ask the partners to decide who will be the "tagger" first. Explain that the person who is "tagger" will chase only their partner. When they tag their partner, they stop and say, "I reached my goal!" Their partner will also stop, count to ten and then he or she will become the tagger.

7. Explain that their partner should use the counting time to get as far away as possible!

8. Explain that you can throw in a twist whenever you feel like it by yelling, "Control!". When you yell "Control!", the tagger and the runner change directions.

Reflection:

1. Were you able to tag or not be tagged all the time? What got in your way?

2. Who had control here?

3. What happened when I said, "Control!"?

4. What are strategies that can help you and your peers develop skills toward empowerment?

. . . .

Let's Win!!!

Estimated Time

15 minutes

Description:

Let's Win is a low-key activity in which students empower each other by finding win-win solutions.

Learning Themes:

- Solve problems by analyzing causes and potential solutions.
- Display an ability to make decisions that support community norms and pro-social behaviors.
- Understand the emotions underlying conflict.
- Develop skills needed for peacefully resolving conflicts in socially acceptable ways.

Props:

- Numerous treats or healthy snacks or other incentives your group enjoys
- Flip chart paper
- Markers

Setup:

None

Framing:

"What does it look like when we are empowered, able to make decisions for ourselves? Think about some positive behaviors we use when we are empowered. Let's list them."

As your students come up with behaviors that they think demonstrate empowerment (taking responsibility, making decisions), list them. This list needn't be all inclusive, but you should challenge anything inappropriate.

"One behavior that I think shows empowerment is finding solutions to problems that are win-win. Let's practice."

Procedure:

1. Generate a list of behaviors that demonstrate empowerment and post it so that it is visible to the entire class.

2. Have students partner up with someone they want to thumb wrestle with for healthy snacks/treats.

3. Students may sit at desks or on the floor as long as there is an even space between partners.

4. Tell the students that each partnership is going to try to win as many treats as possible in 30 seconds. Every time the partner's thumb touches the other person's hand, they win a treat.

5. Review that a win-win situation means that the solution worked for both people versus a win-lose situation where someone misses out.

6. Time a couple of rounds and keep track of the progress, passing out treats as you go.

7. Try one more final round to see if the partnerships grasp that if they cooperate versus compete they both are winners, therefore both people win!

Reflection:

1. Ask pairs to rate their performance in terms of practicing some of the behaviors generated on your list on a scale of zero to five by showing the corresponding number of fingers on one hand. No fingers is awful/no behaviors and five fingers is awesome/a lot of behaviors.

2. Acknowledge the range and highlight positive responders.

3. Explain the win-win approach to conflict resolution and demonstrate with a thumb wrestling partner. (Students voluntarily put both thumbs down and get a treat.)

4. How does win-win relate to control to empowerment? (You may need to prod with: Are both students and teachers winning when students help each other follow the Full Value Contract/Circle of Strength?)

Tip:

The treat doesn't have to be food – just a little motivator that works for you and your students.

Tip:

The win-win approach shifts the conflict resolution approach from one person being right and the other wrong to "I want to win and I want you to win too." This changes disagreements from "right and wrong" situations to cooperative agreements. This approach works because both parties get more of what they want and are committed to the solution.

Pi (π) Charting

Description:

In this quiet activity, students describe that oft-heard word *behavior*.

Learning Themes:

- Manage one's behavior in accordance with the Full Value Contract.
- Describe and demonstrate what it means to be a contributing member of a Full Value community.
- Describe the importance of rules and/or norms of behavior in a Full Value Community.

Props:

- Markers and/or other drawing supplies
- Flip chart or large paper
- Tape

 Estimated Time

15 minutes

 Tip:

Use this activity anytime you want to define a word. Be creative – 'looks like' can be actual drawings, use instruments for 'sounds like', use feelings marketplace cards for 'feels like', etc.

Please note: we have used Pi Charting a couple of times in this book because it is a great way to understand concepts and accommodate differing perceptions. It is always different, especially because the words or concepts being defined change.

Setup:
None

Framing:

"We all use words that we think have the same meaning for everyone, but often they don't. Behavior can be one of those words. Adults use the word behavior a lot. Most of the time it is when you're in trouble, right?"

Take a few seconds to see if heads are nodding, etc.

"But really behavior is good, bad or neutral. Let's make sure we all know what it means. Does behavior look, sound and feel different to us? Let's explore what behavior means to you and what it means to people in our classroom."

Procedure:

1. Explain to your students that the same word may have different meanings for different people.

2. The teacher should write behavior on a piece of paper like this:

BEHAVIOR		
LOOKS LIKE	**FEELS LIKE**	**SOUNDS LIKE**

3. The group then brainstorms what behavior looks like, feels like, and sounds like. There is no right or wrong; this is just how students think of the word. The teacher should jot down anything that comes up. Students can say what comes to their mind, trying not to talk over one another – popcorn style. It is OK if you need to add more structure to this brainstorm through, perhaps, a talking stick or raising hands.

Using *respect* as an example:

- It might *look like* recognizing people when they enter the room or looking at people when they talk to you.
- It might *feel like* you belong or what you have to say matters.
- It might *sound like* people being quiet when others are talking or someone saying "good idea."

4. Once the words are on paper, your students should have a discussion about what's written. This is time for students to explain what they meant, to ask for clarity, and to come to some degree of consensus. You won't want to spend a great deal of time on this, just enough to have a group understanding, but not so much time that your students become bored or disengaged. You will recognize that it's time to stop the discussion when momentum dwindles. (You needn't complete charting a word or all the words in one sitting. Come back to it if attention spans are short.)

Reflection:
What are some ways that our new understanding of behavior could help us in our classroom?

Quality Control

Estimated Time

15 minutes

Description:

In this individual activity, students assess their own behavior.

Learning Themes:

- Demonstrate an ability to evaluate and revise personal and/or group goals.
- Explain how mistakes can be learning experiences and used to help achieve one's goals.
- Describe how one's choices and decisions impact the achievement of goals.
- Describe a positive future for one's self.

Props:

- A copy of the quality control worksheet for each student (found in the Appendix)

Setup:

Give each student a copy of the worksheet.

Framing:

"You are working toward becoming empowered; not relying on teachers to tell you how to act, but following the Full Value Contract on your own. What are some of the ways you can do that?"

Give them time to answer and write on flip chart paper. (Save the flip chart paper for lesson two.)

"One of the ways to become empowered is to honestly understand how you behave right now and figure out how to improve that. Today we are going to start using a worksheet to help us figure out how we are behaving."

Procedure

1. Ask students to complete the quality control worksheet.
2. Circulate through the room to answer questions and challenge self assessments that seem either too positive or negative.

Reflection:

1. What are some of the areas that need your attention?
2. What steps do you need to take in order to raise your score?

Tip:

Use the quality control worksheets as often as you'd like!

3. Who can help you to achieve these steps?
4. Let's keep these in a folder. We will be completing quality control worksheets at least once a week.

Variations

Keep each week's assessment and compile the scores over a month's time to use with treatment plans or as a general measurement of progress.

Where RU on the Scale?

Estimated Time

20 minutes

Description:
In this worksheet-driven activity, students practice giving honest feedback.

Learning Themes:
- Demonstrate the ability to comply with different norms for various settings, i.e., class time, lunch, social/recreation time.
- Manage one's behavior in accordance with the Full Value Contract.
- Demonstrate self-control and the ability to cope with both success and failure.

Props:
- A copy of the Control to Empowerment worksheet for each student (found in the Appendix of this book)

Setup:
Give each student a copy of the worksheet

Framing:
"Today we are going to discuss Simpson's Control to Empowerment Scale. It is a scale that will help us to understand how good we are at controlling our own behaviors and how much we need guidance. Level one means you really need the teachers/staff to help you control your behavior and level ten means you are empowered and controlling your own behavior. Put your peers' names beside the level you think they are on this week. Also jot down an example of their behaviors to let us know why you think that."

Procedure

1. Give your students time to ask questions and clarify their understanding of Control to Empowerment.

2. Hand out worksheets and have each student rate their peers on where they think they are on the scale.

3. Go around the room as your students are working. Help them: 1) attach examples to their ratings; 2) keep their ratings real, no glossing over the bad behavior of a friend and 3) keep their ratings caring – given to help others improve themselves.

4. Compile the worksheets and average all your students' scores.

5. Post the results and discuss.

Reflection:

1. How do you feel about these scores? Are they reflective of the group?

2. How can we get the scores higher next week?

3. What are the specific areas that we need to work on?

4. How do you think Control to Empowerment relates to our Full Value Contract/Circle of Strength?

5. Why do you think it is important to be empowered?

Tip:

When your students are giving feedback, it is important to ensure that no one is becoming a scapegoat. This is one reason that examples are important.

Tip:

These worksheets can be used to average individual scores alone.

Section IV: GRAB

The theme of this section is learning GRAB (Goals, Readiness, Affect, Behavior) as a tool for self assessment.

Activities:

- GRAB-It
- Helium Hoop
- Mastermind Relay

- The Group GRAB
- Transformer Tag

. . . .

GRAB-It

 Estimated Time

30 minutes

Description:
In this fast-paced activity, students begin to identify the GRAB components.

Learning Themes:
- Demonstrate the ability to comply with different norms for various settings, i.e., class time, lunch, social/recreation time.
- Demonstrate social awareness through empathic and caring statements and/or behavior.
- Demonstrate self-control and the ability to cope with both success and failure.

Props:
- 4 note/index cards per student
- At least 1 marker per student

Setup:
Ask the students to gather around a large table or on the floor.

Framing:
"Today we will be learning about another tool for understanding our progress."

Procedure:

1. Give each student four note cards and have them write one word of the GRAB acronym on each card (one word per card). The words are: Goals; Readiness; Affect; Behavior.

2. When complete, have them write on the other side of the card their individual perception of the group as related to each word. Encourage students to not use the GRAB word in their description For example: Readiness – I feel that we are able to listen to each other which means we can go on the field trip we have scheduled for next week.

3. As your students complete the cards, circulate and answer any questions or prompt them by asking them some questions.

3. Collect all of the cards and shuffle them well.

4. Deal out the cards one by one with the acronym word face down and the individual response face up so that all of your students can read it.

5. As the cards are flipped over, read the comment out loud and the first person to identify what category it belongs to gets to GRAB-It.

6. The object is to be first to get one of each of the GRABs cards.

7. Students may not grab the card they created.

8. After someone "wins," play another round.

Tip:

Students will be more likely to ask questions if you are standing/moving among them than if you stand or sit at the front of the room.

Reflection:

1. Were there any confusing GRABs examples?

2. When you look at our responses, does anything stand out as something we need to work on?

3. Is everyone clear on all the aspects of GRAB?

Variation

Post all the cards on a bulletin board and see how fast the entire team can group all of the similar cards together.

Helium Hoop

Estimated Time

30 Minutes (time can vary widely on this activity)

Tip:

This is a great activity to observe, reflect on observations and use observations to assess students.

Description:

Helium Hoop is an often intense activity in which students assess their behavior using GRAB.

Learning Themes:

- Demonstrate self-control and the ability to cope with both success and failure.
- Display an ability to make decisions that support community norms and pro-social behaviors.
- Demonstrate an ability to appropriately express one's needs and emotions.

Props:

- 1 Hula™ type hoop per 10 students

Setup:

None

Framing:

"Sometimes something seems that it should be easy and it is not and surprisingly we find ourselves in very difficult situations. We may feel stuck, overwhelmed, frustrated and want to blame someone else for what is happening. When we ground ourselves by managing our own thoughts, feelings and behaviors, we can get through stressful situations and not be distracted by negativity. The first step to being able to do that is to be aware of your thoughts, feelings and behaviors — as you do this activity, pay attention to yourself."

Procedure:

1. Separate into groups of ten and ask each group of students to stand in a small circle with their index and middle fingers of one hand extended in front of them.

2. Explain to the group that their challenge is to lower the hoop as much as possible with everyone maintaining contact with the hoop at all times. No one may lose contact with the hoop.

3. Place a hoop in the center of the circle and ask students to rest it on the front pads of their index and middle fingers only! Do this after you explain the challenge, because, as you know, as soon as you put it down, the "helium" takes effect and they will not hear the rest of the information!

4. If anyone loses contact with the hoop, simply stop the process, return the hoop to waist height and try again.

5. Ask students to be aware of their communication and focus while participating in this activity.

Reflection:

1. Was it as easy to do as you thought it would be when I gave you the directions? Explain.

2. How did you respond to the difficulty?

3. Was anyone angry?

4. How do you know you were angry? Did you act differently toward your team members?

5. If you found yourself becoming angry, were you surprised by how you felt and acted?

6. How did the work we've done with GRAB help you or your group be aware of its reactions and lower the Helium Hoop?

 Additional Thoughts

• *Because this activity is more difficult than it sounds, it can elicit frustration very quickly. This is often evidenced by blame language. Address feelings as needed.*

• *Groups will move with the hoop horizontally as well as vertically.*

• *The activity can also be finished very quickly. If so, have students switch spots in the circle and use their other hand and try again*

Variation

Instead of a hoop, use a pole/broom handle/etc. The group will form a straight line and interesting communication issues may arise.

Mastermind Relay

Estimated Time

45 minutes

Description:

In this fun problem-solving activity, students use GRAB to assess themselves.

Learning Themes:

- Support each other in achieving goals and making decisions.
- Learn to work together to achieve a common goal or task.
- Demonstrate self-control and the ability to cope with both success and failure.

Props:

- A variety of brainteasers of your choosing – at least four, but feel free to use more (see below for some ideas)
- At least one piece of paper per pair of students
- 1 pen/marker/pencil per student
- 2 pieces of activity rope to mark a start and finish line

Setup:

1. Make stations for each brainteaser and label each station with one of the GRAB components – Goals, Readiness, Affect and Behavior. The stations could be on desks or the like. Allow room for students to circulate. Or give each team a list with materials to work through on their own to minimize sharing information across teams.

2. Mark a start and finish line.

Framing:

"When we solve problems, we are doing something that gives us the opportunity to learn about ourselves – especially when we pay attention. Think about GRAB and use it to assess yourself and your partner. Let's do something and learn about ourselves along the way."

Procedure:

1. Divide your group into teams of pairs.

2. Tell students that this relay requires them to solve the puzzle at each station. Each station is also labeled with one of the GRAB components. Along with solving the puzzle, students should write down concrete examples of how they are doing, as a team of two, on that component. For example, when they reach Readiness they might write: "We are ready to rule or rock the house today." Or "We can get along to set goals that are similar for each other." Or

"We are struggling to keep up with the activity because we are arguing." They move to a new station once you've checked their solution (or you can use the honor system if it is appropriate for your group).

3. They don't need to move in any sequence.

4. Tell them they finish the relay when they cross the finish line.

5. Line them up at the start line and signal "Go!"

6. You may want to ask for fast walking only during this activity.

Reflection:

Reflection Activity:

1. Ask students to stay in small teams and discuss:

   - Did thinking about the GRAB components help you to perform this activity?

   - Give each other some examples of how you think some or any of the GRAB components changed for you individually throughout this activity.

Brainteasers

- A station of Sudoku puzzles torn or copied from a puzzle book – one per team.

- Rearrange six match sticks to make nothing. The match sticks may not be bent, broken or placed over one another. There are two answers that seem worthy of consideration: rearranging the matchsticks into a zero or repositioning the matchsticks into the word NIL. Remember to scatter matchsticks once your answer has been checked.

- If today is Monday, what is the day after the day before the day before tomorrow? Answer: Monday

- Write the number 10 using only nines. Think math! Answer: 9 + (9 ÷ 9) = 10

- Why are 1980 pennies worth more than 1979 pennies? One thousand nine hundred and eighty one cent coins are worth one penny more than one thousand nine hundred and seventy-nine one cent coins.

- Drawing only two straight lines make a box out of the number below:

Answer: (add vertical line to 3 to make a B and a diagonal to the 1 to make an X)

- Excluding this question, how many Fs are in the following sentence?
FEATURE FILMS ARE THE RESULT OF YEARS OF SCIENTIFIC STUDY COMBINED WITH YEARS OF EXPERIENCE. (**Answer:** Six)

Tip:
This self-led reflection will give you an opportunity to listen to the groups and assess their progress in attaining this lesson's learning objectives.

Tip:
Do an internet search for more brainteasers.

The Group GRAB

Estimated Time

15 minutes

Description:

In this worksheet-driven activity, students evaluate their group using GRAB.

Learning Themes:

- Describe and demonstrate what it means to be a contributing member of a Full Value community.
- Describe the importance of rules and/or norms of behavior in a Full Value Community.
- Manage one's behavior in accordance with the Full Value Contract.

Props:

- A Group GRAB worksheet found in the Appendix.

Setup:
None

Framing:
"Let's figure out what we need to do to be a more valuing group using GRAB."

Procedure:

1. Handout the worksheets while explaining that the students will be assessing their current group and commenting with examples.
2. Circulate, answering questions and clarifying as needed. Give students the time they need to complete the worksheet.
3. As the students finish, total the numbers for each of the categories and post the average score for each category in a place where everyone can see them.
4. Have the class share examples of why any score is extremely high or extremely low on the 1-10 scale.

Reflection:

1. What are the areas that need your personal or the group's attention?
2. How can the group gain points for next week?
3. What area should we, as a group, focus on?
4. What are our strategies to keep that focus?

Variation

Do another assessment every month and post the comparative scores in order to show growth or change in group development.

Transformer Tag

Description:

In this fast-paced activity, students explore how assessing themselves and others can help them solve problems better.

Learning Themes:

- Exhibit an ability to accept, acknowledge and appreciate differences.
- Demonstrate social awareness through empathic and caring statements and/or behavior.
- Identify the ways in which having differences on a team helps that team to accomplish its goals.

Props:

- 4 cones or the like to mark boundaries

Estimated Time

10 minutes

Setup:

1. Clear a large, open space in your classroom or use an open space like a gym or field.
2. Set out four cones to mark boundaries for a tag game.

Framing:

"Have you ever tried to download music on a computer or on to a MP3 or iPod? When you are trying to decide on what songs or type of music to download, have you ever noticed how differently you select music than some of your friends? Some people like to pick just one exact song and other people like to pick the whole CD of songs. Well, that's because there are three main approaches to problem solving. Some of us are "thinkers" and like to have a plan. Some of us are "wingers" and like to get in there and try everything out. Some of us are "feelers" and get a feeling about something and go with our gut. It is important to recognize that each of these styles has a place in our group and that one style will be more helpful than the others at certain times. Most of us use all three but each of us has a preference. In this activity, we will explore these three types of problem solving styles"

Procedure:

1. Ask students to form a circle inside the cones.
2. Tell students that they are going to play a tag game in which everyone can tag and no one will be out, but that they will have to start by representing one of three problem-solving styles.
3. Explain that there are some people who are thinkers. They are always think-

ing before they act, have everything planned out and are very organized. They are represented by having their hand on their head.

4. Next, note that there are others who just jump right in and get involved in whatever is happening. They are wingers and are represented by putting their hand on their hip.

5. Finally, there are the people who use their instincts or feelings and act when they get a sense of what is going on. They go with their gut and are represented by putting their hand on their stomach.

6. Ask the class, on the count of three, to represent their favorite problem-solving style by putting their hand on their head, hip or stomach.

7. Say to the students: "In this tag game, you can switch other people over to your style. For example, if my hand is on my head and I tag someone who has a hand on the hip, he or she will have to change to the head." Demonstrate this with someone in the group.

8. Tell the class that you are going to practice fast walking in the cones and the tagging will begin when you hear the word _____ (whatever word you'd like). "Remember, when you hear the word, 'Freeze' – everybody stops where they are."

9. Stop the game when everyone is the same sign…really, it happens!

Reflection:

1. Was anyone surprised by his or her own or someone else's preferred style of problem solving?

2. Does something similar happen when you are trying to make decisions with your friends?

3. Did you think there were times when someone was thinking too much (being too emotional or too quick to decide)? How did you feel when that happened? (For example: Were they frustrated, understanding, patient, etc.)

4. How do you think knowing your own and others' preferred style of problem solving will help us with figuring out what is going on for us as we use GRAB?

Section V: Common Cognitive Distortions

Cognitive distortions have been defined as erroneous or rationalizing attitudes, thoughts, or beliefs concerning one's own or others' behavior.[9] Brooklin Baker of Missouri State Western University states, "Youth, especially delinquent youth, use cognitive distortions to justify socially unacceptable actions as acceptable." Cognitive distortions interfere with a student's ability to accurately assess his or her self or others. They serve to enable one to maintain anti-social behaviors.

The activities in this section are designed to help students identify their own and their group members' cognitive distortions and then use this information to assess self and others.

Activities:

- Asteroids/Ankle Biters
- Last Detail
- See Ya!
- Thinking Errors
- Trust Wave
- Who Am I?

---

9. Liau, A. K., Barriga, A. Q., Gibbs, J. C. (1998). Relations between self-serving cognitive distortions and overt versus covert antisocial behavior in adolescents. Aggressive Behavior, 24: 335-346. http://clearinghouse.missouriwestern.edu/manuscripts/144.asp

Asteroids/Ankle Biters

Estimated Time

25 minutes

Description:

In this version of a tag activity, students will be physically active and reflect on helping themselves versus getting help from others to stay in the activity.

Learning Themes:

- Demonstrate physical self-awareness.
- Exhibit an ability to collaborate as part of a team including leading and following.
- Display an ability to make decisions that support community norms and pro-social behaviors.

Props:

- Fleece balls – one per student

Setup:

Begin by giving one fleece ball to each of the players. Have group members spread themselves out within the defined playing area.

Framing:

"Sometimes we get in a bind and we think other people put us there. Then we sometimes think other people are going to have to get us out or we have to get out of the bind all by ourselves. I have found though that a lot of times it is a combination of both our work and others' help that empowers us to get out of a bind."

Procedure:

1. Give each student a fleece ball.
2. At a designated signal, players start by tossing their balls into the air and allowing them to hit the ground. The play begins with each player picking up any ball from the floor and throwing it, attempting to hit another player below the shoulders.
3. Once hit, a player stoops down and is out. If a ball is in the player's hand when he or she is hit, that ball must be rolled away.
4. The round ends when there is only one player left standing.
5. The second round begins the same as the first round. One additional rule is that if a ball rolls by a squatting player who can reach it, that player can take the ball, get back up, and resume playing.

6. For the third round, add the ankle biter variation. Explain that when you are "out," you have two options. The first remains the same, to grab a loose ball within your reach and to rejoin the activity. The second is to become an ankle biter. This involves staying in your stooped position and reaching out to anyone who gets close enough, and tagging the back of someone's ankle. This frees the biter, and "tags" the thrower.

Reflection:

1. When you were tagged, how did you get out of the bind?
2. Did you have help?
3. How did it feel when you were tagged?
4. Did it make you angry at the person who tagged you? If so, why? Tagging is part of the game, right?

Safety Check

- *Players must stay within the boundaries.*
- *All throwing should be aimed below the waist. Balls may not be caught.*
- *Ankle biters need to be very careful not to get kicked.*
- *Be sure to use soft balls and limit throwing to below the shoulders.*

Last Detail

Description:

This is an activity that provides your students with an opportunity to focus on being present, being aware of others by utilizing their observation skills.

Learning Themes:

- Exhibit an ability to accept, acknowledge and appreciate differences.
- Identify the ways in which having differences on a team helps that team to accomplish its goals.
- Understand what it is to focus on/pay attention to another.

Estimated Time

15 minutes

Framing:

"We are going to experiment today with your ability to see a difference. We will explore being present and staying in tune with the change around you. When you are assessing yourself and others, you are paying attention to the details, so let's practice this with each other."

Procedure:

1. Have each line/team take a good look at the person directly opposite them.
2. Ask each line/team to turn their backs on one another and change one physical thing on their person (e.g., untie a shoe, remove rings, turn glasses upside down).

 Tip:

No peeking! The change needs to be something that can be seen. For example, undoing a button under a sweater wouldn't work.

3. Once everyone has made a change, ask the teams to turn around and face the opposite line in the same place in which they started.

4. Ask teams to take turns guessing what changes were made. You can organize this or not (students could give you answers popcorn style – challenging them to be considerate of one another's talking time – or, for example, raise hands) as best fits their skills and your goals for them.

5. Keep score: each correct answer = +1 and each incorrect answer = -1.

6. Run about three rounds.

Tip:

Observation is critical to a good therapeutic adventure program. Just as your students are working on observation skills, so are you. You need to observe and validate pro-social behavior and confront oppositional, defiant behavior especially as students move from control to empowerment.

Reflection:

1. What were some of the changes you noticed?

2. Was there anything that seemed easy to notice? Why?

3. What observation skills did you use in this activity?

4. How do you use observation skills during a regular day? For example, if you saw your best friend rubbing her eyes what would you think and do? How is that different than if you hadn't noticed?

5. How does that connect to assessing yourself and others?

Variation

In pairs, students try to guess the emotion their partners are trying to express by watching body language only. Hand out index cards with one emotion written on each. When students turn around, they should act out the emotion written on their index card while the opposite team/line tries to guess the emotion they are expressing.

See Ya!

Description:

This activity allows students to learn more about each other – their similarities and differences – in a non-threatening manner.

Learning Themes:

- Exhibit an ability to accept, acknowledge and appreciate differences.
- Demonstrate self-awareness through the expression of thoughts and feelings.
- Demonstrate an ability to appropriately express one's needs and emotions.
- Learn the subtle cues that people use to express their emotions.

Props:

- 10 pieces of webbing or rope 15 feet long (arranged into 10 circles)

Estimated Time

25 minutes

Setup:

1. Develop five to six questions for discussion and five to six questions for determination (see the examples following the procedure).
2. Clear a large space in your classroom.
3. Tie pieces of webbing into a circle. They should be large enough so that three to four students can easily fit inside. You should adjust the number of circles according to your class size (i.e., for a class of 24 students, you'd have six to eight circles).
4. Scatter the circles around a large, open space in your classroom.

Framing:

"Friendships become more important to young people during the teen years. Friendships help us define who we are, offer us a sense of belonging and provide us with support. We want to fit in with and be like our friends. Often, when we try to fit in, we learn how different we are from one another. When we learn about differences, we can fall into stereotyping and prejudice. Pay attention to the changes in your thoughts, feelings and behaviors in response to the different questions during the next activity."

Procedure:

1. Have students separate themselves so that there are three to four players starting in every circle.
2. Begin by asking everyone to introduce themselves to their circle partners.

3. Explain that while the students in each circle might change, the number of people per circle will stay the same.

4. Tell students that no player may leave the circle until they hear the words, "See Ya!" and that the group will say, "See Ya!" after the teacher says, "Ready?" Practice saying "See Ya!" for a few seconds – with feeling

5. Tell your students that people will leave and join their circle. When their circle is joined, they should have the same number of people in it that they began with. So, when one person leaves, your circle will want another person to join.

6. When someone leaves a circle, the remaining students wave their arms and hands up in the air, and shout, "Over here, over here!" until a new student enters their circle – remember always the same number of people per circle. Practice the, "Over heres" for a few seconds – with feeling.

7. Explain that the game will begin with a discussion question, e.g., "Tell each other the last movie you saw and if you liked it or not." Give each small group about 60 seconds to discuss the question.

8. The discussion question will be followed by a determining question such as "Determine who is the tallest in your circle." Give each small group about 15 seconds to respond to the determining question.

9. At the end of the 15 seconds, you will say, "Ready" and the "pre-determined" person (i.e., the tallest person) needs to leave the circle to the sounds of their group saying, "See Ya!" This person must quickly join another circle where the students are saying, "Over here! Over here!"

10. Repeat the process once everyone has a new group and they have introduced themselves.

11. Repeat eight through nine with new questions about five to six times.

Examples of Discussion Questions:
Tell Each Other:

- "If you have ever lived abroad or in a different state, where did you live and what was that like?"
- "Tell your circle about the last book you read and whether or not you liked it."
- "Tell your circle about the oldest person you ever met and what they were/are like."
- "What do you think about music that is usually listened to by cultural groups other than your own?"
- "Tell your circle if you have acted to protect the environment – if so, what you did and what you think about protecting the environment in general."
- "Tell your circle if you have ever spoken up about a comment or "joke" that was feeding stereotypes or prejudice? If you did, tell them what that was like."

Examples of Determining Questions:

Determine who:

- Is the tallest in your group
- Has the shortest hair
- Has the biggest feet
- Is the most flexible
- Has the most siblings
- Has the fewest pets

Reflection:

1. What did you learn about each other?
2. How did it feel when you discussed a topic together as compared to when you had to separate someone from your circle?
3. How did it feel when you had to leave your circle?
4. How did your thoughts, feelings, behaviors change in response to the different questions?
5. What did you learn from this activity that will help you to communicate better with different kinds of people?

Thinking Errors

Estimated Time

15 minutes

Description:

This activity is designed to help students to learn and understand what a thinking error is and utilizes the Thinking Errors worksheet from the Appendix.

Learning Themes:

- Demonstrate self-awareness through the expression of thoughts and feelings.
- Demonstrate responsible and healthy decision-making.
- Solve problems by analyzing causes and potential solutions.

Props:

- 1 copy of the Thinking Errors worksheet (from Appendix)

Setup:

None

Framing:

"Have you ever heard an adult say, 'You don't know what you are thinking'? Or 'You need to examine your thoughts'? Irritating, huh? Well, maybe there is something to that. Let's find out what I mean."

Procedure:

1. Review handout and explain all the thinking errors.
2. Divide your group into small groups of three or four students.
3. Ask the small groups to role play one of the thinking errors to see if the rest of the group can guess which error they are portraying.
4. Repeat as needed until all the thinking errors have been portrayed or for maximum fun!

Reflection:

1. What were some of the thinking errors that were hard to recognize?
2. What thinking errors do you see yourself or others presenting regularly?
3. How can we help each other identify and change these thinking errors?

Variation

Teams of two could compete against each other in a Charades type game

Trust Wave

Description:

This is a dynamic trust activity that requires students to be capable of following directions so that the learning themes may be explored.

Learning Themes:

- Define and demonstrate the ability to give and receive trust.
- Implement decision-making skills, refusal skills and goal setting to avoid risky behavior.
- Support each other in achieving goals and making decisions.
- Know and appreciate one's peers.

Props:

None

 Estimated Time

20 minutes

 Tip:

Monitor your students closely. Trust activities are very powerful but need vigilance to minimize risk.

Setup:

Ask the group to form two lines that face each other. The distance between the two lines should be wide enough for opposing players to stand wrist to wrist if they were to extend their arms in front of them.

Framing:

"Have you ever had to face a scary challenge 'head on' rather than shying away? Sometimes facing our thinking errors is scary. One person – the "jogger" – is given an opportunity to walk, skip or jog all the way down between these two lines. Everyone in line will have their arms stretched out in front of them. Just before the "jogger" hits the arms, they are moved up and out of the way. Each student will select his or her own level of challenge in this activity, so remember the Challenge by Choice philosophy. We are here to support you."

Procedure:

1. Ask for a volunteer to be the jogger.

2. Before the jogger gives his or her commands to ensure that everyone is ready, the students should briefly huddle and come up with a gratitude for the jogger. For example: "We are grateful that Cindy is so honest." They should then say this together to the jogger. This should not be about an external characteristic (looks, money, having a car, etc.), but about a personality trait/social skill (sincerity, listening, understanding, etc.)

3. This jogger should start about ten yards from the head of the two lines. Before 'jogging,' he or she should say at least one thinking error they have used that they plan on stopping/leaving behind. Then the jogger yells, "Ready to walk

(skip or trot)!" – letting the group know that he or she is ready and what speed to expect. He or she does not start until the group responds, "Walk (skip or trot) away."

4. The jogger, using whatever pace is comfortable, approaches the lines *maintaining the same speed throughout the jog or walk.* The spotters (all of the people in the two lines) are positioned with their arms outstretched, heads turned toward the jogger. As the jogger approaches them, and just before it is too late, each pair of spotters raises their arms up so that the jogger passes untouched. This motion looks like a giant wave as it passes down the double line.

5. Have your students practice this motion before the first jogger comes.

6. Students should rotate the line after each jogger. The student at the head of the line should move to the end so that everyone has at least one turn at the head of the line.

7. Allow the jogger a second turn to increase his or her speed if desired.

8. Allow any other student who would like to be the jogger to do so. Encourage everyone to take a turn, but let them know it is their choice.

Reflection:

1. Were you able to trust that the spotters would move in time? Why?

2. Were you able to go faster on your second attempt? Why?

3. What was the perceived risk vs. the actual risk in this activity?

4. Do you think it was easier to jog knowing that people appreciated you?

5. Was anyone surprised or upset by the gratitude he or she got? Can you explain?

6. What thinking errors got left behind? If you were really able to do that, how would your behavior change?

7. How do you think we can help each other eliminate our thinking errors?

8. What does appreciating others' positive qualities have to do with that?

Who Am I?

Description:

This activity focuses on the ability to identify thinking errors and allows students to role play various thinking errors. Students will have needed to be introduced to thinking errors prior to doing this activity. Consider doing the "Thinking Errors" activity prior to this activity.

Learning Themes:

- Analyze potential consequences when confronted with a behavior choice.
- Demonstrate self-awareness through the expression of thoughts and feelings.
- Learn to work together to achieve a common goal or task.

Props:

- Index cards with one thinking error printed on it – one per student
- Masking tape
- Flip chart paper

Estimated Time

20 minutes

Setup:

1. Write the thinking errors on a piece of flip chart paper so your students can see as well as discuss them. (You could have the students brainstorm these with you to generate a list and review at the same time.)
2. Tape a thinking error on each student's back. Be sure he/she doesn't know what it is.

Framing:

"We have had a chance to learn and discuss what thinking errors are. In this activity, you will be trying to guess what thinking error is attached to your back. You will get clues from your peers as they will do their best to demonstrate the thinking error by role playing an example of the thinking error on the card attached to your back. Have fun and be creative in your role play examples but don't give away the name of the thinking error by accident!"

Procedure:

1. Be sure that each student has a thinking error taped to his or her back. No one should know what that characteristic is.
2. Students are to discover which one of the characteristics is on their back by watching their peers "act out" the thinking error with words and/or actions.

3. When someone reads your card, they can only act out one scenario to help you figure out your characteristic.

4. No additional questions can be asked or answered.

5. When students correctly identify the thinking error on their backs, they can wear their cards on the front.

6. The activity continues until everyone has identified their thinking error.

Reflection:

1. What was it like to try to guess your thinking error?

2. Did you see anyone behaving as you might sometimes?

3. What was the thinking error that you thought was the hardest to guess/act?

4. Can you describe any strategies you have that help with your own thinking errors?

Variations

• *Have your students select a card and role play the thinking error on it before you conduct the above activity so they have some examples to chose from.*

• *Ask students to get into partnerships and then select a thinking error card. Tell them not to show it to the rest of the class, but determine a scenario that depicts that thinking error. When ready, have them role play the thinking error to the rest of the class and see if they can determine which one it is.*

Section VI:
Reassessing the Full Value Contract

The theme of this section is reassessing how the group is doing on the Full Value Contract. Also, use this as a time to fortify your FVC with students' new insights.

> **Activities:**
> - Circle the Circle
> - Metaphor Creation
> - Wearing Someone Else's Glasses

· ·

Circle the Circle

> **Description:**
> This activity focuses on students working together to solve a problem while trying to care for themselves and others.
>
> **Learning Themes:**
> - Describe and demonstrate what it means to be a contributing member of a Full Value community.
> - Demonstrate social awareness through empathic and caring statements and/or behavior.
>
> **Props:**
> - 2 Hula™ type hoops

Estimated Time

15 minutes

Setup:
None

Framing:
"We have established behavioral goals for our group – our Full Value Contract (Circle of Strength). Life can move quickly, but even so, it is important to remember to care for ourselves and others. Let's remind ourselves of how we do it!"

Procedure:
1. Ask the students to hold hands with the person next to them and to form a big circle.

Tip:

Did your students demonstrate good listening skills? If so, point it out – point out when they didn't listen too. Reflect on what happened as well as making the connection from framing to reflection.

2. Place one large hoop between two students (resting on their grasped hands).

3. Explain to the students that they are to try to get the hoop around the circle as quickly as possible without letting go of hands.

4. Next, increase the challenge by adding the second hoop. The hoops will move in opposite directions around the circle (over the students), eventually crossing over each other and returning to the starting point.

Reflection:

Reflection Activity:

1. Give each person a 5 x 7 inch index card. Have them rank from one to five (five is excellent and one is poor) – first how well the group helped solve the problem of getting the hoop(s) around the circle and secondly how well the group cared for themselves and one another, physically, while passing the hoop. They can spread out to do this. Give them a few minutes.

2. Come together as a large group and ask individuals to explain what criteria they used to determine their ranking.

3. Finally, ask each student to complete a sentence on their card. The sentence is: In regard to Respecting Myself and Others, today I learned (students should fill in this blank) ..

Additional Thoughts

Be sure that the hoops are large enough for everyone to successfully pass through.

Variation

For an added challenge, you can time this activity.

Metaphor Creation

Description:

Metaphor Creation is an activity in which students will create a three-dimensional representation of their Full Value Contract. (Note how we have provided ways for multiple learning styles to learn about and explore Full Value.)

Learning Themes:

- Describe and demonstrate what it means to be a contributing member of a Full Value community.
- Exhibit an ability to collaborate as part of a team including leading and following.
- Understand and describe how the Full Value Contract can be an asset to their community.

Props:

- Different types of 3-D art supplies – examples include: pipe cleaners, masking tape, cardboard rolls, foam shapes, cardboard.

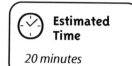

Estimated Time

20 minutes

Setup:

Keep your Full Value Contract/Circle of Strength and Contract Garden hung prominently on the wall in the room in which you're working.

Framing:

"Our Full Value Contract is a living document. It changes, grows and develops as we do in our community. It allows us to add and subtract those items that we feel will be most helpful to us in achieving our individual and group goals. In this activity, we want to continue to develop and refine what our Full Value Contract means to us. We will be creating a sculpture or three-dimensional object that represents the behaviors we are working toward so that we can continue to grow as a community."

Procedure:

1. Instruct the students to come up with a tangible 3-D item that could represent their group and their Full Value Contract.

2. Once the item is agreed upon, bring out the art supplies and instruct the students to create it in a form that can be carried along to other classrooms (sturdy and reasonable size).

3. After the project is complete, have the students add the items of the values they have shown on the inside and the detractors of their group on the outside. Be sure to stay with the theme of the item chosen.

4. The last stage is for everyone to sign the item so they understand that they are re-committing to their group and their values.

Reflection:

1. How well have we represented all of our previous Full Value Contracts?

2. Did everyone participate and stay involved with this process?

3. What are some of the more difficult values to uphold? Did we experience any of those while creating this 3-D sculpture?

4. What are the applications of these values to the entire school?

Variations

• *Examples of a good 3-D object can be given to reduce the time needed to accomplish this lesson (i.e., backpack, tool box, fortune cookie).*

• *Use clay and have the class either create a clay sculpture or have individuals create their own personal sculptures representing what the Full Value Contract looks like to them. Present the sculpture(s) and discuss.*

Wearing Someone Else's Glasses

Description:

This is a worksheet-driven activity that requires observation in feedback skills. It is designed to improve self awareness in relation to the Full Value Contract.

Learning Themes:

- Exhibit an ability to accept, acknowledge and appreciate differences.
- Demonstrate social awareness through empathic and caring statements and/or behavior.
- Demonstrate and practice the ability to give and receive healthy feedback.

Props:

- A copy of the 'wearing someone else's glasses' worksheet for each student (from Appendix)

⏱ **Estimated Time**

20 minutes

Setup:

None

Procedure:

1. Give each student a worksheet and a pen/pencil/marker.
2. Have the students walk around to their peers and collect feedback – examples of how they have demonstrated the values listed on the Contract/Circle of Strength.
3. Once completed, share examples with the group and post students' worksheets.

Reflection:

1. Explain how difficult or easy it is to receive feedback on your performance.
2. What comments, questions or concerns do you have regarding the feedback you received?

Chapter Three:

Working and Collaborating
with a Team

This chapter builds on the community and assessment skills we've worked on so far to further develop social skills and emotional intelligence critical to a student's ability to be a functional and contributing member of society. This unit reinforces some of the important skills described by Daniel Goleman as part of the emotional competence framework[11] promoted through the activities in the other chapters such as:

- Communication
- Understanding others
- Developing others
- Leveraging diversity
- Leadership
- Conflict management

This chapter expands on these by focusing on the following skills (also from Goleman's framework):

- Collaboration and cooperation
- Team capabilities
- Initiating and managing change
- Building bonds
- Influence

Young people tend to spend a lot of time with their peers. This time is often focused on "goals such as affiliation, having fun and social positioning."[12] Young people need structured time to help develop the skills that Goleman has defined.[13] The activities in this chapter have been designed to help young people experience, reflect on and begin to replicate those skills.

It is worth noting that most of the activities in this guide ask students to employ teamwork. Use the following activities to reinforce work you've already done or to introduce the skills and outcomes that we have focused on.

We will be looking at teamwork in the following ways: defining good teamwork, how students contribute to the team and developing and accomplishing shared goals. We will be viewing collaboration as: goal partners – getting necessary support and supporting others in achieving individual goals and understanding the difference between collaboration and competition.

11. Goleman, Daniel (1998) *Working with Emotional Intelligence*, Bantam Dell; New York, New York
12. Larson, Reed (2007) From I to We: The Development of the Capacity for Teamwork in Youth Programs; in Silbereisen & Lerner, (eds) (2007) *Approaches to Positive Youth Development*, Sage Publications; Los Angeles, California; pp 278-279
13. Ibid

Section I: Defining Teamwork

Everyone knows it is important to be able to work well as a team, but what does that mean? Your students may throw the word teamwork, or the like, around without being really clear about its meaning. Or it means one thing to them and another to you or someone else. We have a clear idea of the skills that encompass teamwork, skills we want our students to develop. It is critical that we share those with our students so they know what is expected of them. The activities in this section are designed to do just that.

Activities:

- Car and Driver
- Escher Dilemma
- Hoop Relay
- Object Retrieval
- Pi Chart Teamwork
- Teamwork Speed Rabbit

Car and Driver

Estimated Time

15 minutes

Safety Check

- *Make sure students are ready for this activity!*
- *Play in an area that is free of obstacles.*

Description:
This fun pairs activity helps students define collaboration.

Learning Themes:
- Define and/or demonstrate the ability to compromise.
- Exhibit an ability to collaborate as part of a team including leading and following.

Props:
- Cones, game ropes or the like to delineate a road

Setup:
Set up a series of cones, or the like, to represent a road for cars and drivers to use.

Framing:
"Driving a car can be a lot of fun, but it is a lot of responsibility as well. You have to keep yourself, your passengers and the people around your car safe! Today you will be driving a very expensive car. Your job is to be a responsible driver."

Procedure:

1. Before introducing the rules of this game, ask the students what they think the safety considerations should be for playing a game with their eyes closed? (Slow pace, Bumpers Up as you are able, etc.)

2. Before introducing the rules, have each student describe what kind of a car they feel like being today. For example: "I feel like a Mac truck today, strong and powerful."

3. Separate your students into pairs. For odd-sized groups, either join in yourself or have the group of three take turns doing the activity in pairs.

4. Have the students set themselves up so that one student is in front of the other. The student in front is the car, and the student in back is the driver.

5. Drivers will guide their cars by placing their hands on the shoulders of the cars, as well as by using verbal communication.

6. Once students are in the course, you can offer the students who are cars a blindfold or simply ask them to close their eyes.

7. Give your students a couple of minutes to strategize with their partners. They will want to try to figure out: how they will know to turn left or right; speed up or slow down, etc.

8. Have the students enter the pre-set course so that there is at least 15 feet of space between partners.

9. Drivers are to safely (without hitting anything) drive their cars through the course.

10. Once students have completed the course, have them switch roles so that everyone has a turn being the driver or the car.

Reflection:

1. Did the teams of cars and drivers work together, if so how? Or did the driver just try to manage everything when it was his or her turn?

2. Was it a lot to manage?

3. Collaboration means working well together with others. Can you list four ways that drivers and cars collaborated with each other?

4. Can you tell me about four ways that we can collaborate with each other in our program?

Variations

• Have teams of three or more – car, driver and passenger(s). The whole team needs to stay connected.

• Change the types of driving conditions such as: highway = straight and fast movement with passing permitted; country roads = winding in and out of each others' paths; city roads = stopping and turning every few steps.

Escher Dilemma

Estimated Time

20 minutes

Description:

This low-key team activity focuses on clarifying the meaning of roles on a team.

Learning Themes:

- Demonstrate an ability to ask questions, negotiate, and support team decisions.
- Exhibit an ability to collaborate as part of a team including leading and following.
- Define and/or demonstrate the ability to compromise.
- Demonstrate self control and the ability to cope with both success and failure.

Props:

- Escher Dilemma Kit*
- 1 rules card per student (See Setup.)

Setup:

1. Write one of the following six rules on an index/note card. Prepare at least one set of the basic six rules below. Make enough copies of each rule so that everyone gets one. It is OK if someone has more than one rule in their possession as this will stimulate more conversation in problem solving the activity. It is fine if there are multiple copies of a rule in use.

   RULES

   - Your team must use all fifteen pieces.
   - The puzzle is a triangle.
   - Pieces of the same color may not touch each other in the final assembly.
   - The triangle must be equal on all sides.
   - There can be only one puzzle when your team is finished.
   - There can't be any gaps or holes in the completed puzzle.

2. Have the puzzle pieces ready in a bag or the like.

Framing:

"You each have one (or at least one) piece of information that you need to contribute to solving this puzzle. You may share the information on your card verbal-

---

* Available from Project Adventure

ly, but you may not show the card to anyone. Do your best to solve this problem and we will see how long this takes you."

Procedure:

1. Hand out the rule cards as described in the Setup.
2. Give your students access to the puzzle pieces.
3. Time them.

Reflection:

1. How did you figure out what all the rules were?
2. Did knowing that I was timing you make the task easier, harder or was it inconsequential? Did that add stress to your teamwork?
3. Did different people have different roles? If so, what were they?
4. Did you have any difficulties working together? If so, what were they? How did you resolve them?
5. How did you work well together? Can you give examples?
6. What do you think we should keep in mind as we keep on working together?
7. How can we use the skills we've highlighted here?

Variations

- *Make it easier: Print all the rules on one sheet and give them to everyone.*
- *Make it harder: Students cannot tell or show each other the rule on their card. This is a good test of their Be Honest skills.*

Hoop Relay

Estimated Time

15 minutes

Description:

This moderate activity helps students focus on how they contribute to a team.

Learning Themes:

- Demonstrate self-control and the ability to cope with both success and failure.
- Exhibit an ability to collaborate as part of a team including leading and following.
- Demonstrate an ability to ask questions, negotiate, and support team decisions.

Props:

- 4-6 Hula™ type hoops
- 1 can Play Doh™, lump of clay or the like per two students

Setup:

None

Tip:

If holding hands is an issue, little sections of rope can be held onto by students to form an attached line. In this case, it will be one student holding a short piece of rope with the next student holding the other end of that short piece of rope.

Framing:

"Sometimes when we work together, each individual needs to contribute in the same way. We don't get the chance to choose who can do something based on how good they are at it. We all just have to pitch in and do the same work together to get the job done. However, we can still be really strong team members."

Procedure:

1. Separate your group into two teams. Each team should select someone to start the hoops. The hoop starter will be joining the action after all of the hoops have been started.

2. Have the teams form lines. The team members should hold hands except for the hoop starter. The hoop starter faces their team.

3. Explain that each team will need to pass the hoops along their line until the person at the front is back at the front. These are the rules:

   - People in the line must hold hands.
   - Upon your "Go" the hoop starter will start a hoop by placing it over the head of the first person in line.
   - When the first hoop is on the fourth person, the next will start until each team has started both or all three of the hoops.

- When all of the hoops are started, the hoop starter should join the line at the front.
- When a hoop reaches the last person, the last person should run to the front and start that hoop again. Remember to continue to hold hands.
- Each team is finished when the original first person is back to the front again.

4. Give each team their hoops. You'll give them two or three depending on how challenging you want the activity to be or how large the group is. Three hoops is a bigger challenge for a smaller group and will keep a larger group more engaged.

5. Start the action.

Reflection:

Reflection Activity:

1. Everyone should find a partner from the other team. A group of three is fine!

2. Give each partnership a can of Play Doh™, lump of clay or the like.

3. Ask the partnerships to create a sculpture that represents one way they contributed to their team and one issue they think they struggled with and maybe slowed the team down or didn't support their team members as much as they would have liked. This is one sculpture representing a contribution and a challenge they both had.

4. Each partnership will present this sculpture to the larger group explaining the shared contribution and challenge it represents.

Variation

- *Don't separate your students into teams. Circle up instead. Time them so they can compete against the clock.*

Tip:

Be sure your hoops are big enough for all your students to fit through.

Tip:

You are, essentially, asking the partnerships to debrief each other. So, you really want them to talk about what happened and find out what they share. This is a good time for you to circulate and communicate your observations.

Tip:

The reflection here doesn't explore competition, but you could. You didn't tell the two teams they were competing, but were they?

Object Retrieval

Estimated Time

35 minutes

Description:

In Object Retrieval, students will have a fairly active experience that reflects upon the different aspects of teamwork.

Learning Themes:

- Demonstrate self-control and the ability to cope with both success and failure.
- Identify the characteristics of leadership and teamwork.
- Demonstrate an ability to ask questions, negotiate, and support team decisions.

Props:

Object Retrieval Kit*

Setup:

1. Create a circle using the boundary rope. The circle can be 10 to 25 feet in diameter. [Note: Test the size of the circle by laying two of the ropes in the kit that students will use to move the buckets end to end through the middle of the circle. There should be one to two feet of rope outside the boundary circle on both ends of the rope.]

2. Place the two spot markers in the center of the circle, approximately 8-12 inches apart.

3. Fill one bucket with balls (typically the more balls in the bucket, the more difficult the solution becomes). Place the full bucket on one spot marker. Place the empty bucket on the other spot marker.

4. Place the other props outside the boundary circle on the ground.

Framing:

"A lot goes into being a team that gets things done. Today we have lots of little tadpoles we need to keep safe. You see, the tadpoles are safe in this bucket, but they will soon outgrow the bucket which is surrounded by toxic waste (point to the area inside the boundary marker). You need to move them to this empty bucket surrounded by a frog-friendly swamp."

---

* Available from Project Adventure

Tip:

Although tadpoles are fantastical, it is more important to protect a bucket of living things than a bucket of balls. The tadpoles add both fun and responsibility to this activity. As always, feel free to substitute a more familiar critter (or critically needed medicine, or qualities/attributes that the group needs to work on etc.) for tadpoles.

Procedure:

1. Ask your students to name some of the ways we get things done as a team. Spend a few minutes discussing these.

2. Give each student at least one ball, a marker and a piece of masking tape.

3. Have them write one way we get things done as a team on the piece of masking tape that goes on their ball (tadpole).

4. Read the labels as you place the balls/tadpoles into the bucket.

5. Put all the balls into one of the buckets.

6. This full bucket should be placed back on one of the spot markers in your boundary area – as explained in the Setup section for this activity.

7. The objective is for the group to transfer all of the balls from the full bucket into the empty bucket. The empty bucket must be on its spot marker when the transfer occurs.

8. The boundary rope and the spot markers may not be moved.

9. No person may touch the ground or extend a body part over the boundary marker. If this occurs, the team must start again (i.e., your students must remove any props from within the circle).

10. Only the props provided may be used to transfer the objects.

11. At no time may any of the ideas (tadpoles/ balls), be moved outside the containment circle.

Reflection:

Reflection Activity:

1. Ask your students to form a circle.

2. Ask a volunteer to stand in the middle. He or she will pull, without looking, one ball/tadpole from the bucket.

3. He or she will read it silently. Then, he or she will approach someone in the circle and read the way we get things done as a team as it is written on that ball. The person who is read to has 10 seconds (you can time or the group can count) to give an example of that. The example can be from the activity or 'real life.'

4. If the person in the middle gets an answer he or she thinks is fishy, they will have ten seconds to call "Challenge."

 Tip:

Adjust the time to increase or decrease the challenge and/or meet the needs of your group.

5. If challenged, the group decides (voting or consensus – you decide) whether or not it is a good example.

6. The person in the middle swaps places with the student in question if no example is given within the time limit or a challenge is lost.

7. Repeat the cycle until or before interest is lost.

· ·

Pi (π) Chart Teamwork

Estimated Time

15 minutes

Description:
This quiet activity will help your students get on the same page regarding what teamwork is.

Learning Themes:
- Identify the characteristics of leadership and teamwork.
- Demonstrate an ability to ask questions, negotiate, and support team decisions.

Props:
- Markers and/or other drawing supplies
- Flip chart or large paper
- Tape

Setup:
None

Framing:
"We just completed a problem-solving activity. We experienced and then talked about teamwork. Let's think more about what teamwork means to us."

Procedure:
1. Explain to your students that the same word may have different meanings for different people.
2. The teacher should write Teamwork on a piece of paper like this:

TEAMWORK		
LOOKS LIKE	**FEELS LIKE**	**SOUNDS LIKE**

3. The group then brainstorms what teamwork looks like, feels like, and sounds like. There is no right or wrong; this is just how people think of the word. The teacher should write anything that comes up. Students can just say what comes to mind, trying not to talk over each other – the popcorn style. It is OK if you need to add more structure to this brainstorm through, perhaps, a talking stick or raising hands.

Using the word teamwork as an example:

- It might *look like* people standing in a circle listening to what someone is saying.
- It might *feel like* you belong or that what you have to say matters.
- It might *sound like* people being quiet when others are talking or someone saying "good idea!"

4. Once the words are on paper, your students should have a discussion about what's written. This is time for students to explain what they meant, to ask for clarity, and to come to some degree of consensus. You won't want to spend a great deal of time on this, just enough to have a group understand, and agree on some common language, actions and feelings but not so much time that your students become bored or disengaged. You will recognize that it's time to stop the discussion when momentum dwindles.

Tip:

Ask students to think about the role of conflict in teamwork. Get them to think about how conflict is not always a bad thing.

Reflection:

None needed; Pi Charting itself is reflective.

Variations

• *As a reflection, ask students to write in their journals for 10 minutes or so about how teamwork is or can be used in the classroom.*

Teamwork Speed Rabbit

Estimated Time

15 minutes

Description:

This quick and fun activity will help reinforce the definition of teamwork, particularly for kinesthetic learners.

Learning Themes:
- Learn to work together to achieve a common goal or task.
- Define and/or demonstrate the ability to compromise.
- Understand what it is to focus on/pay attention to another.

Props:

None

Setup:

None

Framing:

"We have been talking about teamwork. Can you describe it through a sculpture made of three people?"

Tip:

Have fun with the demonstration of this activity, and fully participate with the students to role model enjoyable, zany behavior. It sets a lighthearted tone and reinforces the message that it is OK to try new things.

Procedure:

1. Divide the group into teams of three. A team of four is fine, but they will be creating three person sculptures.

2. Ask each team to come up with (1) a word or two that describes teamwork and (2) a three-person statue that demonstrates that word. (Check the following variation if you need a better understanding of what the 'sculpture' is like. You may want to demonstrate one of those animal sculptures to your students.)

3. Have each team say their word and demonstrate their statue. If two or more teams have the same word, help them find a new one to describe teamwork and the sculpture they already have. Encourage everyone to pay attention to the demonstrations of the three-person statues as they will need to be able to create them in the activity.

4. Choose one person to be in the center of the circle. He or she turns around the circle and then randomly points to someone in the circle and calls out one of the teamwork words. This student counts to five or 10, depending on how difficult you want to make the game.

5. The person who is pointed to becomes the middle of the statue; the people who are on either side of this player are the two sides of the chosen teamwork word. They must try to arrange themselves into the statue before the student in the middle finishes counting to five (or 10). If they don't, the part of the statue that is not in place takes the spot in the middle of the circle. If they are done in time, the student in the middle stays there.

Reflection:
None needed.

> **Tip:**
>
> *Remember to always reflect if something happens that you feel students need to discuss or if someone is upset.*

Variations

• *The plain old, but very fun, Speed Rabbit (find it also in the Project Adventure publication Adventure Curriculum for Physical Education: Elementary School). This activity actually involves a rabbit! Teams of three make animal sculptures starting with:*

> *Elephant – Center person extends left arm down and holds nose with right hand to form a trunk. Side people form ears by facing the center person and making a C shape with their arms.*

> *Rabbit – Center person uses hands to make rabbit ears on his or her head. Side people each stand near the center person while making a fast stomping /stepping motion with their legs like a rabbit.*

> *Giraffe – Center person reaches up into the air above their head, forming the long neck and head of the giraffe. Side people bend over towards the middle person, forming the legs.*

• *Have students add more animals of their own creation once they get the hang of it..*

Section II: How I Contribute to My Team

In the introduction, we outlined Albert Bandura's work on efficacy. In very truncated form, it says, 'When I believe that I am capable of doing something, I can do it.' He further espouses that the best way to feel efficacious is to experience success. This section focuses on helping students use their experiences of being on a team to reinforce their strengths, buttress their weaknesses and help them to feel efficacious about their abilities to contribute to a team. When students believe in themselves – their abilities and skills – they are more likely to perform and utilize those skills. When it comes to teamwork and the interpersonal skills that contribute to the development of a team, we want to provide experiences that allow for success and mastery of those skills. This process is further validated in Reed Larson's Approaches to Youth Development in which he describes learning through experience as one of the most common ways youth learn about teamwork.[14]

Activities:
- Alphabet Soup – Fastback
- Call of the Pride
- Gotcha
- Hi Lo Yo
- Pipeline

14. Larson, Reed (2007) From I to We: The Development of the Capacity for Teamwork in Youth Programs; in Silbereisen & Lerner, (eds) (2007) Approaches to Positive Youth Development; Sage Publications; Los Angeles, California; p.285

Alphabet Soup – Fastback

Estimated Time

30 minutes

Description:

This fast-paced team activity asks students to reflect on their role on a team.

Learning Themes:

- Define and/or demonstrate the ability to compromise.
- Support each other in achieving goals and making decisions.
- Exhibit an ability to collaborate as part of a team including leading and following.
- Demonstrate an ability to ask questions, negotiate, and support team decisions.

Props:

- Alphabet Soup Kit?*
- Ropes for boundary marking
- A stopwatch

Setup:

1. Create three zones as shown in the diagram below.

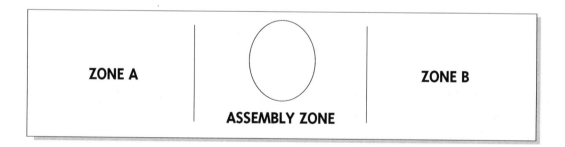

2. The distance from Zones A and B to the Assembly Zone can range from 5-10 feet to 10-20 yards depending on how much running around you want your students to do.
3. Place all the foam blocks (with the cutouts removed) in Zone A.
4. Place all the cutouts of the letters and numbers in Zone B.
5. Make the Assembly Zone midway between Zones A and B.

---

* Available from Project Adventure

Tip:

You could show your students an example of how you'd like the blocks to be assembled or have part of their challenge be figuring out your verbal instructions. The strategy that best suits the needs and goals of your students is the one to use!

Framing:

"Sometimes life gets complicated and I need to pause and reflect on how I contribute to my team. Sometimes I even may need to take on a different role in order to support the group. Let's use this puzzle to look at our roles and our contributions."

Procedure:

1. Tell your students that they are going to assemble the blocks so that alternating letters and numbers are right side up and upside down.

2. Separate your students into two relatively equal roles:
   - **The Assemblers** who must stay in the Assembly Zone at all times to put letter and number cutouts into blocks in the pattern you've specified
   - **The Resourcers** who can move back and forth from Zones A and B to the Assembly Zone, but may not enter the Assembly Zone at any time

3. When the time starts, Resourcers may bring letters, numbers and cutouts to the Assembly area. Resourcers may only carry one piece at a time to prevent work-related injuries and not overwhelm the assemblers. If a Resourcer carries more than one object, he or she must return the objects to the start Zone and then take a 30-second recovery break.

4. Resourcers may place the objects they carry inside the Assembly Zone. They may not help assemble the letters or step into the Assembly Zone. If either of these infractions occurs, the entire operation must stop for 10 seconds.

5. Assemblers may not reach outside of the Assembly Zone at any time. Whenever an arm or a leg or any body part crosses the boundary, a 10-second work stoppage will occur.

6. When assembling the blocks into the final shape – if blocks that should remain separated touch each other – four blocks will be removed from the assembly area and the pieces must be returned to either Zone A or B (depending on whether they are a cut-out or a block) before they can be reused.

7. Give your group five minutes or so to plan and clarify the rules.

8. Start the action and time it.

9. Upon completion, let the students know how well they did on time.

Tip:

You can write the questions on a black board or flip chart or give each group a handout.

Reflection:

Reflection Activity:

1. Keep the teams in the Assemblers and Resourcers groups.

2. Ask them to discuss and report out to the group their answers to the following questions:
   - What did you enjoy about being an _____ (Assembler or a Resourcer)?
   - What did you find frustrating about being an _____ (Assembler or a Resourcer)?

- What do you think your group did well?
- What do you think your group could improve on?
- Overall, how do you think the larger team did?
- Did people have specific roles within their groups? If so, what were they?
- What roles and responsibilities do we have on our team or in our classroom that helps us to be successful and reach our goals?

3. Give students five to ten minutes and report out to the group.

Variations

- *Use your imagination and create your own variations: try assembling the blocks by colors – arrange so all like-colored blocks touch; no like-colored block touches another of the same color; spell words, etc. There are many other possibilities.*
- *This could also be an activity about life skills, getting paid and putting money in the bank, watching it collect and grow into something*

Call of the Pride

Description:

In this activity, students express pride in themselves and their peers.

Learning Themes:

- Understand what it is to focus on/pay attention to another.
- Demonstrate and practice the ability to give and receive healthy feedback.
- Exhibit an ability to accept, acknowledge and appreciate differences.
- Demonstrate social awareness through empathic and caring statements and/or behavior.

Props:

None

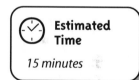

Estimated Time

15 minutes

Setup:
None

Framing:

"We have lots of ways of demonstrating positive qualities on a team, right?" Give some examples of positive things that happened in this lesson's previous activities or something else recent. "Part of good teamwork is recognizing when you and others do something well."

Procedure:

1. Ask the students to get into two lines facing one another inside the open space.

2. Ask students to reach one hand out to the person across from them in order to form pairs.

3. Each pair needs to come up with two words, one that is the name of a quality and the other that is a behavior that demonstrates that quality, e.g., *helpful* and *listening*, or *reliable* and *on-time*. These should be a quality either one or both members are proud to have. Each person in the pair takes one of the two words.

4. The pairs should now split up, returning to their lines. Ask one line of students to go to one end of the room and the other line to the other end.

5. If the two members of the pairs are lined up directly across from each other, you may want to have a line "scramble up" before proceeding with the directions.

6. Ask all students to close their eyes and put their hands in front of their chests (Bumpers Up). On "Go," the lines begin walking toward one another as players call out their partner's words, while at the same time listening for their partners, who are calling out their other words.

7. Students continue calling their partners' words until they find each other. Once they have found each other, they can open their eyes and watch the other students as they search for their partners.

Reflection:

1. What did it feel like to do this activity?

2. How did you focus so that you could find your partner?

3. How do you know what qualities are in different people when you can't "see" them?

4. Can you tell us about the quality you chose and why?

5. What should we think about if we want to show pride in ourselves and not make others feel badly as we build our team?

Gotcha

Description:

In this low-key activity, students share a laugh.

Learning Themes:

- Exhibit an ability to collaborate as part of a team including leading and following.
- Demonstrate an ability to ask questions, negotiate, and support team decisions.

Props:

None

Estimated Time

5 minutes

Setup:
Ask the class to stand in a tight circle.

Framing:
"We have been talking a lot about what makes a good team. You know what we sometimes forget that is really important for a good team to have? Fun!"

Procedure:

1. Ask students to put their right hands, palms facing up, in front of the stomach of the person to their right.

2. Next, ask them to take their left index finger and point it into the middle of the palm that is now in front of their own stomach.

3. Explain that on the count of three they have two tasks: to catch the finger in their right palm, and to keep their own left index finger free by pulling it away from the catching hand of the person next to them.

4. Count to three. Watch students have fun with catching or missing. Then tell students that if they catch someone, they can turn to them and say, "Gotcha!"

5. After a few rounds, you may ask different students to count to three. You may also want to point out the simple rule of "no cupping" which involves not allowing students to cup their hands in order to have a better chance to catch the fingers in their palms.

Reflection:
None needed

> **Variations**
>
> • *Change hands to left hand out in front of the person to your left, and right index finger in the palm in front of your stomach.*
>
> • *Rather than having palms facing up, have palms start higher in the air and face down, with index finger pointing up!*

Hi Lo Yo

Estimated Time

10 minutes

> **Description:**
> In this moderate activity, students explore what it is to be distracted.
>
> **Learning Themes:**
> • Identify the effects of leadership on teamwork and team members.
> • Know and practice strategies for resisting negative peer pressure.
> • Understand what it is to focus on/pay attention to another.
>
> **Props:**
> None

Setup:
None

Framing:
"Sometimes you can just be having fun with your team and someone else can make it hard to do that. Sometimes I will have something on my mind which is distracting me from being a good contributor to my team. Sometimes my actions get in the way of me being successful and sometimes how I act leads directly to success. Let's see how that plays out in this activity."

Procedure:

1. Gather your students into a circle.
2. Tell them that, for this game, there are three words each accompanied by a hand motion. These need to be in order:
   • "Hi" is signaled by raising your hand over your head and pointing at the person to your left or right.

- "Lo" is signaled by lowering your hand as low as you can go without bending and pointing at the person to your left or right.

- "Yo" is signaled by making a two-handed slicing motion toward anyone in the circle (it needs to be really clear who is being signaled).

3. Let them know that the student being pointed at needs to say the next word and do the next motion. So if you get pointed at by someone saying "Yo," you need to say "Hi" and do the motion.

4. Run a practice round for a minute or two and let them get a feel for the rules and the flow.

5. Let your students know that in the 'for real' game, there will be distractions. When someone goofs up on the Hi, Lo, Yo order or motion, they become distracters. Distracters stand outside the circle. Remaining students form a tighter circle. Distracters act goofy, make loud noises and generally try to distract those remaining in the circle. Of course, distracters cannot touch people in the circle and need to keep their language, etc appropriate.

6. The round ends when there are three students remaining in the middle or the distracters are becoming bored.

7. Play another round if there is interest.

Reflection:

1. What are some of the things that distract you from being a strong member of your team? (Point out when some of those have nothing to do with the team.)

2. Do you think there are times when you unintentionally (or maybe intentionally) distract your team mates? Can you share some examples with us?

3. Do you think there are times when you help your team mates be more focused, less distracted? Can you share some examples with us?

4. Ask questions two and three again, but ask them to think about others.

 Tip:

Remember, a really important way that students learn about how they are in a group is by hearing it from others – not just through introspection.

Pipeline

Description:
In this intense challenge, students appreciate their own and others' skills.

Learning Themes:
- Exhibit an ability to collaborate as part of a team including leading and following.
- Demonstrate an ability to appropriately express one's needs and emotions.
- Describe or demonstrate the benefits of positive and challenging goals.
- Learn to work together to achieve a common goal or task.

Props:
- Pipeline Kit*
- Several lengths of rope
- Masking tape
- Markers

Setup:
1. Create a long, curvy pathway with the ropes that will create boundaries for the group to stay within. Any shape that works for your space is fine!
2. Place mesh bag or container from Pipeline kit at the far end of the pathway.
3. Prep the Pipeline pipe pieces by lining the bottom (underside) of each with a length of masking tape.
4. Have three balls from your kit handy (varying sizes are great).

Framing:
"When we work as a team, we use many skills to get the job done. You will be amazed. Pay attention to the skills you and others use as you complete this challenging activity."

Procedure:
1. Ask students to gather in a circle at the entrance to your Pipeline pathway.
2. Pass a piece of prepped Pipeline to each student.
3. Pass a marker to each student.
4. Ask the students to brainstorm skills they use to accomplish goals on a team. Discuss them briefly and select three (some examples might be: listening, sharing ideas, following through, etc.). If you have balls of varying sizes, use

---

* Available from Project Adventure

the largest ball to represent the skill that is the least challenging to use, the second largest to represent the next most challenging skill and the smallest, the most challenging skill. It is fine if you don't have varying ball sizes. It furthers your metaphor to align the most challenging ball with the most challenging skill, but it is not necessary.

Tip:

Feel free to be creative with your pipeline pathway. It can go in and out of rooms, etc. You can make this activity more or less challenging by the complexity of the pathway.

5. Have students identify the possible sources of support available to them in those situations by writing a different one on the masking tape in each piece of Pipeline. (Some examples of support are: sharing concerns, asking for help, offering help, etc.)

6. The class's goal is to successfully travel through the pathway, from entrance to safe home, using their skills (as represented by the balls) while carrying them only by their support (as represented by the Pipeline pieces).

7. Pipeline pieces cannot touch each other. The balls can only travel forward and not stop.

8. Only one ball can travel at a time.

9. If a ball falls to the floor or rolls backward or stops, it begins again – back to the start.

10. Once past the starting line, students cannot touch the balls.

Reflection:

Reflection Activity:

1. Separate your students into three small groups.

2. Lay out the I Am About Cards.*

3. Assign each group one of the three skills represented by each of the three balls.

4. Ask each group to tell the story of each skill's experience in pipeline. They are going to present this story to the whole group and can use one to three of the I Am About Cards to tell it.

5. Give them five to ten minutes to prepare their stories.

6. Have them present their stories.

Variation

• *Vary the rules to decrease the frustration factor – allow them one drop per ball, allow no stopping of the ball – only forward movement etc.*

---

* Available from Project Adventure

Section III: Developing and Accomplishing Shared Goals

The theme of this section is helping students develop, get support for and support others in accomplishing shared goals. This is fundamental to getting things done when participating on a team.

It is not just the students' sense of accomplishment that is being developed through shared goals, but their sense of belonging and camaraderie. Belonging and camaraderie help a student feel committed to/invested in the norms and values of their community.

Please note that this section reinforces work you may have done in the Full Value Chapter. Use this previous work as a building block and foundation.

Activities:
- Change Up
- Community Walk
- Hoop Delight
- Mass Pass
- Willow in the Wind

Change Up

> **Estimated Time**
>
> *30 minutes*

Description:

In this moderate activity, students support the group in attaining goals and begin to understand how they do that.

Learning Themes:

- Identify the characteristics of leadership and teamwork.
- Demonstrate an ability to ask questions, negotiate, and support team decisions.
- Learn to express one's feelings verbally.
- Define and/or demonstrate the ability to compromise.

Props:

- Change Up cards* (set of cards numbered from 1 – 24)
- A stopwatch

Framing:

"Your group will be given a series of challenges. After each challenge is identified, your group will have several opportunities to plan and find solutions. The team goal is to execute the solution as efficiently as possible. You will decide on a good goal for efficiency – you'll tell me what you think a good time is. Once you have had a chance to improve on your solution, a new challenge will be presented. Each time a change occurs, the group will attempt to develop a plan that will help them to accomplish the team goal."

Procedure:

1. Tell your students that you are going to hand out a card and they should not look at it.
2. Hand a card to each student. (It doesn't matter if the numbers selected are sequential, as long as each student has a card.)
3. Remind your students that the goal is to develop and implement a solution as quickly as possible and that they will be timed on this. Tell them that they must signal you once they have finished the task so that you can stop the time.
4. Tell students that challenge number one is to turn their cards over and *line up in numerical order* from the smallest to largest number.
5. Have them make their first attempt and time it.
6. After they have finished, tell your students what they accomplished for time on this attempt – this time is their first benchmark.

---

* Available from Project Adventure

7. Give them a few minutes of planning time to refine their solution and set a goal for how long it will take them in the next attempt. Let them know that they will have a different card in the next round/attempt.

8. Ask them to shuffle the cards by having each person trade cards at least three times with someone different without looking at the cards. Once they get a card to keep, instruct them to refrain from looking at it until told to do so.

9. Remind your students that the challenge is the same as before, the numbers are the same; the only thing that is different is who is holding the number.

10. Give them the start signal and time the solution. Report the time to them.

11. Allow one to two more attempts until your students think they have achieved a good time, shuffling the cards between each attempt.

12. Make a change by announcing Challenge Two, which is to line up *alphabetically* by the first letter of the number on the card they are holding. So the number "eight" would come before the number "eighteen" then "four" and so on. Say "Start" and time the attempt.

13. Report the time to the group. Repeat procedures seven through ten as appropriate.

14. Make another change by announcing Challenge Three which is to line up in two lines – *odd numbers in one line, even numbers in the other – odds in descending order and evens in ascending order numerically.*

15. Report the time to your students. Repeat procedures seven through ten as appropriate.

Reflection:

1. What strategies did your team develop to reach your goals?

2. Did you have individual as well as team strategies to reach your goals? If so, can you tell us what your strategy was and how it helped the team?

3. What was the consequence(s) of change during the activity? Was it different if the changes were "minor" (i.e., shuffling the cards, but the same numbers were always in use) or "major" (i.e., changing from lining up numerically to lining up alphabetically)?

4. What are some ways that we as a team can handle changes that come up in our classroom?

Variations

- *If the group is larger than 24, the activity works well with sub-teams. Each sub-team has its own set of cards but the entire group does the activity at the same time.*

- *Challenge Three can be creative. Create whatever order you want. What has worked well is asking students to line up in a different configuration (odds and evens, two circles, etc.) than in the previous two challenges.*

- *Use a deck of cards.*

Community Walk

Description:
Community Walk is a blindfolded/unsighted activity in which students give, ask for and receive help.

Learning Themes:
- Learn to express one's feelings verbally.
- Define and demonstrate the ability to give and receive trust.
- Define and identify ways of caring for and helping self and others.
- Exhibit an ability to collaborate as part of a team including leading and following.

Props:
- 1 blindfold for each student
- 1 index/note card per student
- 1 pen, marker or other writing instrument per student

 Estimated Time

20 minutes

Setup:
Have an interesting location and direction in mind for a blindfolded walk that matches your group's ability to be challenged as well as the time you have available. (Read through the entire activity including the variations to get a sense of what will work. Remember, just being blindfolded while walking is challenging!) You will lead your students who will all be blindfolded or closing their eyes, looking down, etc.

Framing:
"We are going to be there for each other as we take a challenging walk, one in which you cannot see. Take a moment to share with a partner a goal you might set for yourself in doing this activity. It could be: to wear a blindfold, to do only what you're instructed to do or to trust the leader. Let's really take our time and be safe during this activity."

 Tip:

Feel free to add to or subtract from the time limits we have provided here to suit your needs. You can stop and come back to activities. It is important, even if you stop in the middle, to spend some time reflecting on what happened at the stopping point for every activity to prevent students from having emotional needs that aren't attended to.

Procedure:

1. Have students gather into groups of four to discuss what they will each need from the group to make participating in this activity comfortable and to share what their goals are. Have each student write what they need on an index/note card. Bring the groups together to share what they discussed and begin the activity.

2. Collect these cards and bring them with you as the group has their walk. You will use the cards for reflection.

3. Hand out the blindfolds. Ask students to get into a line and put on the blindfolds.

4. Remind students that while they are walking, there is no talking, but they can be in physical contact with others.

5. Ask the group if they would like to discuss any strategies for proceeding.

6. When everyone is ready to go, take the hand of the first student in line, and begin the walk.

7. Remember to take them in many different directions, over and under obstacles, etc. Make the walk challenging.

8. Stop every few minutes and have the student at the front of the line find his or her way to the end of the line. Be sure that everyone has a turn at the front and the end of the line.

Reflection:

1. How did the group support each other during the activity?

2. Give examples of specific requests and how they were or were not met.

3. How did you support your peers?

4. Is being able to support others a skill you have?

5. How did it feel being the leader and why?

6. How did it feel being the follower and why?

7. I didn't give you a goal for this activity, but did anyone have anything in mind? Can you share that with us? (If needed, your goal can be really simple, e.g., not tripping.)

Reflection Activity:

8. Hand back each student's index card and discuss whether or not they got what they needed.

 Additional Thoughts

• *You can ask one or two students to be sighted spotters and observers of the group.*

• *The more complex the walk, the more risk that students will experience. However, safety is more important than a complex walk!*

Variations

• *If you have a large group, you can separate your students into two or more groups and have a student lead each of the lines. Be sure to switch leaders occasionally to allow for another perspective, that of leader and that of follower.*

• *Have pairs help each other travel blindfolded to another place without touching each other, using only their voices to communicate.*

• *Have students rotate through the front of the line and each lead the group while sighted.*

Hoop Delight

Estimated Time

10 minutes

Description:

This variation on musical chairs explores what students have in common.

Learning Themes:

• Demonstrate social awareness through empathic and caring statements and/or behavior.

• Listen to the feedback of one's peers.

• Know and appreciate one's peers.

Props:

• 1 hoop or loop of rope per three students – big enough for three to stand in

• A CD player, radio or the like

• 1 index/note card per student

• 1 pen, pencil or marker per student

• A hat, bucket, bowl or the like

Setup:

1. Clear some space.

2. Place hoops or rope loops throughout the space.

Framing:

"Have you ever played musical chairs? Well Hoop Delight is very much like that with a slight twist – we will get to know one another a little better and no one is Out."

Tip:

You could randomly join, as being the music master allows, a hoop group. Let your students get to know you too.

Procedure:

1. Tell your students that the hoops are like the chairs in musical chairs. You are going to play music and when it stops they need to find a hoop to stand in.

2. There can be no more than three students in a hoop.

3. There must be at least one new student in the group each time they get to a new hoop.

4. When your students get to a new hoop, give them a minute or so to find one thing they have in common. Keep the music stopped while they discuss their commonalities.

5. Start the music and start the activity – have them find their first hoop.

6. Stop playing when everyone has had at least one turn with each of the other students. However, feel free to keep going if your students are still engaged! You will need to either give them a fresh start or keep going, but eliminate the new student rule (number 3 above).

Reflection:

Reflection Activity:

1. Give each student an index/note card and a pencil pen or marker.

2. Have them write their name on it and throw it into a hat, bucket, bowl or the like.

3. Mix up the cards and have each student draw one, making sure that they do not get their own name.

4. When each student has an index card, have them share one thing that they have in common with the student on their card.

Questions for Discussion:

1. Why do you think it is important to know the people on your team?

2. Is it easier to set and accomplish team goals when you know each other? If so, why?

Variation

Use Hoop Delight as a prelude to Natural Disasters, page 75.

Mass Pass

Description:

In this intense initiative, students explore the balance between group and individual goals.

Learning Themes:

- Demonstrate an ability to ask questions, negotiate, and support team decisions.
- Describe how one's choices and decisions impact the achievement of goals.
- Support each other in achieving goals and making decisions.
- Describe the skills needed to set healthy personal and/or group goals.

Props:

- 1 Mass Pass kit*
- A stopwatch

Estimated Time

45 minutes

Tip:

Before starting Mass Pass, you could have students write their individual goals on a piece of masking tape that they stick to an object. This will make the metaphor more concrete.

Setup:

- Create a fairly large square 15 to 25 feet per side. It is helpful, but not completely necessary, for the boundary markers to enclose the square. However, it is important that *all of the corners* be clearly marked and easily identified.
- In one corner of the square, place one container, and at the opposite corner, place the other container. Place all of the objects inside the first container (the "start" for the activity).
- A typical setup is to have a variety of tossable objects with various levels of difficulty. You get a point for each object that ends up in the second bucket.
- For a group of 15 students, 10 to 15 objects would be appropriate.

Framing:

"People on your team have their own individual goals. Each goal is represented by an object in the 'start' container. To help each other successfully accomplish individual goals, team members must transport them to the "completion" container. So, in this activity, our team goal is to nurture our individual goals. You will have a total of three rounds to implement your solution while being timed. You will be trying to continuously improve your results in each round and to achieve your best score possible in the last round."

---

* Available from Project Adventure

Tip:

Including a variety of objects adds to the challenge. Choose objects that are small and large, easy and difficult to throw, unusual and funny. Just remember that the objects may be thrown, so keep safety in mind.

Procedure:

1. Let your students know that they will be given a total of 40 minutes to complete the task. The time is structured; the first 15 minutes is planning and practice. After the planning session, the clock begins for the first round. Each of the three rounds has a fixed time limit during which your students will try to score the most points they can. Depending on the size of the group, 60 seconds per round is typically enough time. Between rounds, there is an additional five minute planning session.

2. Like many of our activities, this one has plenty of rules (You may want to give your students these rules in writing or post them on the wall.):

   • Students play Mass Pass outside the boundaries.

   • All objects or individual goals must start inside the "start" container at the beginning of every round.

   • The time for each round starts when the first object/goal is removed from the container.

   • All sides of the square must be occupied by at least one student.

   • Once a student has chosen a side, he or she may not switch sides within a round.

   • Each student must touch the object after it leaves the start container and before it lands in the "completion" container.

   • Objects may not be passed to anyone on their immediate right or left, in other words the object must "skip" at least one person when it is passed.

   • Points are earned for each object that is placed successfully inside the completion container after it has journeyed through the team.

   • Whenever an object is being passed from one side of the square to another, it must cross over the inside of the boundary area (i.e., it cannot be passed around the corner on the outside of the perimeter of the square).

   • Any time an object is dropped, it must return to the start container to be recycled, if it is to be used in the round.

   • If an object is dropped inside the boundary markers, it may not be retrieved and is lost for the duration of that round.

   • No member of the team may step inside the perimeter boundary during a round. If such a touch occurs, all the objects must be returned to the start.

3. Give your students some time to ask questions before beginning the action as described.

Reflection:

1. Can you share your individual goals with the group?

2. Was it hard to take care of your individual goals while trying to get the best time possible? If so, why?

3. How do you think we can accomplish our team goals while supporting ourselves and each other in achieving our individual goals?

4. Have you ever had times when it was hard to accomplish your individual goals because they were in conflict with what your group or team wanted? Can you describe that for us?

5. What should we do to help balance team and individual goals?

Variation

Any kind of polygon will work for this activity. The more sides, the more challenging it tends to be.

Willow in the Wind

Description:

In this trust activity, students explore the role of trust in being on a team.

Learning Themes:

- Demonstrate physical self-awareness.
- Define and identify ways of caring for and helping self and others.
- Define and demonstrate the ability to give and receive trust.
- Demonstrate an ability to appropriately express one's needs and emotions.

Props:

None

 Estimated Time

20 minutes

Safety Check

- *Challenge by Choice is essential in this activity.*
- *A group of 12 to 14 is usually about the maximum number of active students. Otherwise the circles get too large for the leaners to safely lean. If your group is bigger, separate into small groups, ensuring that they do not run the activity without appropriate supervision..*

Please note: It is important to be aware of the safety issues of this activity and have a group that is responsible and able to pay attention before attempting this activity.

Setup:
Members of group should stand in a circle.

Framing:
"We are going to practice being respectful. Think of both what you need to be respected and what you give to others to help them be respected. Keep those thoughts to yourself for now. One way we show ourselves and those around us respect is to pay attention to what you're doing and how it affects others. I think you're ready to do this, do you?"

Procedure:

1. Ask a volunteer to stand in the middle. This person, as the leaner, must have arms crossed over the chest, feet planted solidly on the ground, body stiff.

2. The spotters around the circle need to stand close together, shoulder to shoulder (or elbow to elbow if their height is varied). There should be no gaps in the circle where the leaner could slip through.

3. Before getting a volunteer to lean, ask everyone to say at least one thing they do/give to others to demonstrate respect.

4. Before leaning, the leaner should state at least five things received from others that makes him or her feel respected. They should identify anything else they need from the group when leaning.

5. The group should use the lean commands:
   - *Leaner: "Team, are you ready to respect me?"*
   - *Spotters: "Ready."*
   - *Leaner: "Leaning."*
   - *Spotters: "OK. Lean."*

6. The leaner may lean in any direction. The group is to pass the leaner gently around in a random pattern.

7. Stress that no one person should ever be the only one holding the leaner; there should always be multiple people with hands on the leaner.

Reflection:

1. How did we do? Did everyone feel safe?

2. Were there a lot of similarities in what people need and give to show respect? Any surprises?

3. When you told the group what you needed to feel respected, did it feel like you were being respectful of yourself?

4. How do you think respecting yourself and others is important to accomplishing team goals?

5. What are some other ways that people show that they have respect for themselves?

Tip:

Always stop an activity if you feel it is unsafe (physically or emotionally). Then, lead a reflection on what happened that was unsafe and what the group can do to be safe next time. Sometimes this kind of experience can be a valuable, teachable moment.

Additional Thoughts

• *You may ask students to be silent while a person is being passed around. This can help to maintain emotional safety by reducing unwanted comments.*

Section IV: Goal Partners

The theme of this section is helping students to find partners to support them in accomplishing their individual goals as well as giving and receiving feedback. This section will either further develop work you have done previously or help your students as it is.

> **Activities:**
> - Body Guard
> - Goal Partner Check In
> - Goal Partner Check Out
> - Help Me Tag
> - Key Position
> - Keypunch
> - Twist and Turn

- -

Body Guard

Description:

In this playful activity, students explore what it means to be responsible for another person.

Learning Themes:

- Learn to express one's feelings verbally.
- Demonstrate an ability to appropriately express one's needs and emotions.
- Support each other in achieving goals and making decisions.

Props:

- 1 fleece ball or soft tossable for each student
- I Am About Cards*

Estimated Time

15 minutes

Tip:

We have inserted current expressions such as "got your back" here to encourage you to use current language. Don't use this language if you wouldn't naturally!

Setup:
None needed

Framing:

"Sometimes your goal buddy will have your back and sometimes you'll have theirs."

---

* Available from Project Adventure

Procedure:

1. Have your students form a circle.
2. Ask for one pair of goal partners to volunteer to be the first pair in the middle.
3. Ask one of the pair to be Tag and the other to be Body Guard.
4. Give the students forming the circle one soft tossable.
5. Explain that they are going to be trying to tag Tag by hitting him or her with a tossable/fleece ball. Body Guard is going to try to protect Tag from being tagged by deflecting the ball you toss underhand at him or her.
   - Body Guard cannot touch anyone or cover up Tag completely.
   - Tag and Body Guard need to stay inside the circle.
   - The group remains in a circle.
6. When Tag is hit, the goal partners will switch roles.
7. When both have been hit, a new pair of goal partners comes into the middle.
8. If you have a three-member goal partnership, ask for one member to volunteer to play twice. Three people in the middle will make tagging one unreasonably hard or tagging two too easy.
9. Play until everyone has had a turn at each role.

Reflection:

Reflection Activity:

1. Spread out the I Am About Cards.
2. Have everyone pick a card that shows how it felt to be Tag.
3. Go around the circle and have everyone show their cards and explain why they picked them.
4. Ask your students to return their cards. Shuffle them around.
5. Repeat three and four for Body Guard.

Variations

When Tag is hit, the person who hits Tag becomes Body Guard. Although this variation does not further explore goal buddies, it provides a great opportunity to discuss how sometimes we "get" people and sometimes we are "there" for them.

Goal Partner Check In

Description:

In this check in, students begin to establish a structure of supporting each other in attaining goals.

Learning Themes:

- Support each other in achieving goals and making decisions.
- Describe the skills needed to set healthy personal and/or group goals.
- Demonstrate an ability to appropriately express one's needs and emotions.

Props:

- Goal Partner worksheet (from the Appendix)

Estimated Time

5 minutes

Setup:
None

Framing:
"We all have individual goals that we are working on in our school (program/ agency/etc.). Today we are going to find a partner to help us set and accomplish our goals. Once you have completed the SMART Goal worksheet, you will share it with a partner."

Procedure:

1. Have students find partners to share their goals with. A group of three is fine.

2. Give each student a copy of the Goal Partner worksheet.

3. Explain that they will be filling them out for today's activities only. So, for example, a goal of 'I will not swear during today's class' will work. A goal of 'I will only swear three times this week' will not.

4. Remind them to make sure their goals are SMART as the worksheet directs and to sign their own sheets as well as their partners'.

5. Let them know that you are going to collect the sheets so they can check in with their goal partners again at the end of the lesson.

6. Circulate and answer questions and make suggestions for appropriate goals as needed.

Reflection:
None needed

Goal Partner Check Out

Estimated Time

5 minutes

Description:

In this check out, students begin to establish a structure of supporting each other in attaining goals.

Learning Themes:

- Support each other in achieving goals and making decisions.
- Describe the skills needed to set healthy personal and/or group goals.
- Demonstrate an ability to appropriately express one's needs and emotions.

Props:

- Completed Goal Partner worksheets, from Check In

Setup:
None

Procedure:

1. Return Goal Partner worksheets to their owners

2. Ask the partners to find a quiet space to check on whether or not goals were accomplished. Remind them to be honest with each other. They are trying to help each other grow, not be stuck in the same pattern. Conversely, honest feedback should be given in a caring manner so their goal partners can hear it and do something about it, not be overwhelmed and react to not feeling cared for.

3. Circulate and join the partners as needed, but try to let the partnerships work by themselves.

Reflection:
None needed

 Tips:

The Goal Partner Check In and Out are intended to be bookend lessons. It is helpful to bookend your week or day with brief goal partner checks like these. They help students to set and accomplish goals, build community and provide rituals.

Help Me Tag

Description:
In this fun activity, students explore the need for asking for help.

Learning Themes:

- Demonstrate an ability to appropriately express one's needs and emotions.
- Define and identify ways of caring for and helping self and others.
- Demonstrate social awareness through empathic and caring statements and/or behavior.

Props:

- 1-3 rubber chickens*
- Boundary markers (ropes, cones, etc.)

Estimated Time

15 minutes

Setup:
Create a boundary that is large enough to allow for some running – about half of a basketball court for 20 students. The area should be flat and free of obstacles.

Framing:
None needed

Tip:

Sometimes it is good to just play and reflect on what happened during the activity. However, it is important to ensure the physical and emotional safety of your students so make sure you say what you need to about safety!

Procedure:

1. Select one student (or more depending on group size) to be It.
2. Give the rubber chicken (or more depending on group size) to another student.
3. The person who is It will try to tag other students. Tags are allowed on the back of the shoulder only.
4. Anyone holding the rubber chicken may not be tagged. Only one person may have the chicken at a time. The student holding the chicken may not move.
5. A student who has been tagged must kneel down in the spot where they were tagged.
6. Someone who has been tagged can be thrown the rubber chicken to get back in the activity. Yelling, "Help me! Help me!" is a good way to get the chicken carrier's attention. If this student gets the carrier's attention and catches the rubber chicken, he or she may rejoin the activity. If the student does not catch the chicken, he or she may not pick up the chicken. Any student still in the activity may pick up a dropped chicken and use it as he/she wishes.

7. Any student may handle the rubber chicken except for the person who is It.

8. Switch the It student every five minutes or so. Check the student's affect and switch as the It student becomes tired.

Reflection:

Reflection Activity:

1. Were you able to ask for help and how did you help others?

2. How did your ability to ask for help change when faced with the pressure of being tagged?

3. What does asking for help have to do with keeping each other safe?

Key Position

Estimated Time

15 minutes

> **Description:**
> In this activity, students learn about their assets.
>
> **Learning Themes:**
> • Support each other in achieving goals and making decisions.
> • Demonstrate social awareness through empathic and caring statements and/or behaviors.
> • Evaluate and observe the behaviors, attributes and strengths of others.
>
> **Props:**
> • 1 spot marker per student – use those in the Keypunch kit*
> • 1 sticky note per student (you may want some extras on hand)
> • 1 pen or marker per student

Setup:
Place one spot marker per student on the ground in a circle.

Framing:
"One way we get what we need and give others what they need to accomplish their goals is to know and let others know what we are good at."

Procedure:

1. Away from the circle of spots, give each student a sticky note and a marker.

---

* Available from Project Adventure

2. Ask them to write one strength that they have – one that helps them to achieve goals and that they have used to help others achieve goals. Let them know that they will ultimately be sharing with the group, but should keep it to themselves for now.

3. Give them a minute or so to do that. Have them hand the notes back to you when they are done. (If a student is stuck, quietly help them. Don't let the other students hear.)

4. Stick the notes underneath the spot markers. The spot markers should remain in a circle.

5. Invite your students to stand on the spot markers, one on each.

6. Then, have them look at the strength written on the sticky note beneath them.

7. If it is their note, they should stick it on their body (Keep it appropriate please!) and remain on their spot.

8. If it is not their note, they should stick it back under their spot marker and invite the person they think that strength belongs to, to stand on that spot. They should then move to that person's spot

9. Repeat seven, eight and nine until everyone has their own note stuck to their bodies.

Reflection:

1. How easy was it to come up with your strength?

2. How was it to have someone suggest that they knew one of your strengths?

3. Why do you think that knowing your strengths will help you and others to achieve goals?

4. How are we resources for ourselves and each other?

5. How should we share our strengths with each other?

Reflection Activity:

Strength Bombardment

1. Give each student 30 seconds to be bombarded by their strengths.

2. Ask a volunteer to go first.

3. His or her peers have 30 seconds to bombard the volunteer with their non-physical strengths. Students are free to talk over each other – you only have 30 seconds to get it all in! So they are saying things like: "Strong!" "Kind!" "Determined!"

4. The volunteer/recipient's responsibility is to simply receive the compliments and say, "Thank you."

Keypunch

Estimated Time

25 minutes

Description:

In this fast-paced initiative, students work on setting and revising goals.

Learning Themes:

- Describe the skills needed to set healthy personal and/or group goals.
- Learn to work together to achieve a common goal or task.
- Demonstrate an ability to evaluate and revise personal and/or group goals.

Props:

- A Keypunch Kit*, boundary rope or other cord/rope

Setup:

1. Create a small play area, about five by ten feet, using the boundary cord in the Keypunch Kit.
2. Randomly place spots, with numbers up, in this space.
3. Make a start line about ten feet away from this play area.

Framing:

"You all know how to count to 30, right? We are going to work on doing that as a team today. Keep the strengths that you bring to your team in mind as you work together."

Procedure:

1. Gather your students beyond the start line.
2. Let them know that they will be trying to touch the spots in numerical sequence, one through 30. But there are rules:
   - If spots are touched out of sequence, the group starts over.
   - Only one person is allowed beyond the start line at a time.
   - There is no talking once the first person has crossed the start line.
   - Everyone must have a turn.
3. Let them have a practice run and time it.
4. When they have finished, let them know their time.
5. Let them know that all planning must be done behind the start line.
6. Give your students a few minutes to plan and set a time goal.

* Available from Project Adventure

7. Start the action.

8. Repeat until your students are satisfied with their accomplishments.

Reflection:

Reflection Activity:

1. Ask your students to walk over to the circle and pick a number from one to 30 that best represents how they did achieving group and individual goals. One is bad and 30 is awesome. Ask them to do this as a group. They may share numbers. They should be prepared to tell you why they picked that particular number.

2. Tell them you will know they are ready when they have picked the Keypunch spot marker with that number on it.

3. Discuss why they chose that number.

Question for Discussion:

1. Ask each student to give you an example of how they brought a strength to the activity. (This can be the strength they named in Key Position or not.)

Variations

• Like Alphabet Soup, the number combinations are limitless. You can switch it up to make the activity more or less challenging.

• Let your students talk during the activity to make it less challenging.

Twist and Turn

Estimated Time

45 minutes

Tip:

We have found that a 40-foot long rope is a good size for a group of 10 or so. If your class size is 15 or more students, your rope will need to be longer so that everyone will have a hand in making it work.

Description:

In this intense initiative, students try not to get frustrated as they work to achieve a group goal while keeping their individual goals in mind.

Learning Themes:

- Demonstrate an ability to evaluate and revise personal and/or group goals.
- Learn to work together to achieve a common goal or task.
- Demonstrate self-awareness through the expression of thoughts and feelings.
- Demonstrate self-control and the ability to cope with both success and failure.

Props:

- Game frame*
- 40-80 feet of rope
- Colored tape

Setup:

1. Set up the game frame.
1. Mark the rope with a piece of colored tape every four feet or so.
2. Divide the group in half and have each half go to opposite sides of the web/game frame.

Framing:

"We have a challenge today. We have to weave our individual goals, as represented by this rope, into our shared team goals, as represented by this web."

Procedure:

1. Let your students know the rules for weaving the rope:
   - Students must remain on the side of the web that they start on.
   - The rope needs to be entirely off the ground before they start.
   - The rope must go through every opening to complete the weaving.
   - The rope cannot go more than four feet through an opening before it has to go through another one (No more than four feet of rope can build up

* Available from Project Adventure

on one side before it has to pass through another opening. Let your students know you've marked the rope at four foot lengths.).

- The rope cannot touch the web; if it does, the rope must go back through three holes and start again.
- The rope cannot touch the floor; if it does, the rope must start over again.
- No one can touch the web; if they do, they must start the rope over again.

2. Tell them they have completed the task when the back end of the rope is successfully through the last hole.

3. Let them know that you are expecting them to be honest about when they have broken a rule.

Tip:

If your group has a low tolerance for frustration, then starting over may be too much. If there is a touch, simply have your students back the rope through the last one or two holes instead.

Reflection:

Reflection Activity:

1. Separate your students into three or four teams.

2. The small teams should convince you that the weaving they just made using the game frame and rope is awesome.

3. To do this, each small team should write and perform a jingle. The jingle should let you know about (1) all the strengths in the weaving and (2) how much work went into it.

4. Let them know that they don't have to sing their jingle, but they should creatively perform it!

5. Give the small teams five minutes or so to write and prepare the performance of their jingle.

6. Go around and have each team perform their jingle. Start the clapping and cheering after each performance.

Chapter Four:
Acquiring Leadership Skills

The Collaborative for Academic, Social, and Emotional Learning (CASEL)[15] states that effective Social and Emotional Learning programs should work on developing five core social and emotional competencies in students: Self Awareness, Social Awareness, Self Management, Relationship Skills and Responsible Decision Making. We have chosen to specifically focus on three of these competencies in this chapter as it relates to Leadership. Leadership requires Self Awareness, Social Awareness and Responsible Decision Making. The other two competencies – Relationship Skills and Self Management – are included inherently in the nature and structure of the activities in this chapter. As with many of the activities in this book, by changing the focus of the framing and the reflection questions, the impact and learning from the activities shifts toward other competencies as desired. Empathy is a sub-component of Social Awareness. We have chosen to focus a significant portion of the framing and reflection questions on this sub-component as we have found it to be a vital area for our students as they develop as leaders.

Being a positive leader or follower and knowing when the use of each skill set is required is pivotal for young people with behavioral problems. Many of the young people we consider to be at-risk are often leaders, but not in a positive way. So, they often have leadership skills, but are either not applying them or don't know how to apply them appropriately. We have focused the activities in this section on the development of social emotional skills in areas, which experience has shown us, need bolstering among at-risk students:

- Self Awareness (Defining leadership) – What is the difference between a positive and a negative leader? What do positive leaders do? How do I become a positive leader? When is it OK to be a follower? Am I the leader of my life?

- Responsible Decision Making – How do I make decisions that enable me to use my leadership skills positively? How do our decisions match our values (ethics)?

- Social Awareness – Empathy – How do I offer care and compassion and still get things done? How are others feeling? What must it be like to be in someone else's situation? Does helping others make me a leader?

This activity guide is written with the assumption that students need to possess the skills to both lead and to follow. You as a facilitator will need to take the basic reflections from these activities and grow them into larger conversations and lessons that more deeply explore the bigger questions cited above.

The focus of Project Adventure activities is for young people to move toward a feeling of empowerment and competence (self efficacy). By building leadership skills, encouraging responsible decision making and raising social awareness, you are helping to develop the skills that empower your students to be assets to their communities (family, school, etc.). You are also guiding them so that they begin to

---

15. *Safe and Sound: An educational reader's guide to evidence-based social and emotional learning (SEL) programs:* Collaborative for Academic, Social, and Emotional Learning, Chicago, IL, 2003.

see that they are capable and competent and can make meaningful contributions to their own life and the lives of others. It is also vital to understand that it is not just you, but their peers telling them that they are capable and competent!

Through the following activities, encourage your students to explore these leadership and, to some degree, followership issues. Look for ways to help students gain confidence in themselves and begin to identify and replicate effective strategies for leading and following.

For more in-depth explorations of leadership, see Project Adventure's *Adventure Curriculum for Physical Education* (select the age level that works for you).

Section I:
Self Awareness - Defining Leadership

In order to develop leadership skills, one must understand and experience what it means to lead – to be able to look around the world and see different leaders and leadership styles and then begin to integrate this information into one's self awareness. "What qualities, skills, attributes do leaders have that I want to have?" In other words, before your students can become positive leaders, they need to know what a positive leader is and begin to discover what qualities and competencies they possess. This takes self reflection and feedback from peers. It requires taking the time to gain insight into one's strengths and limitations. This section is focused on gaining this insight and feedback. Students will ask themselves and others, "What is a leader? Can I be one? Do I already have some of the skills and qualities needed to be a good leader?"

When one is a positive leader, is it about being able to have people do what you tell them to do? Does being a positive leader involve listening and being empathetic and letting others take the lead?

In some ways, it is equally as important, when defining leadership, to define what it takes to be a good follower. Developing self awareness in this area helps to balance the understanding of what leadership is. Are you a good follower when you do as you're told? Or is it more complex than that? Do you have to consider what is healthy for you and those around you before following? Does a good follower need to challenge leaders if they have made a decision with which he or she disagrees? Does a follower have power?

Although these are seemingly simple and obvious questions, the definition of leadership among young people needs to be challenged in order to grow into one that empowers both the leader and the follower. The following activities have been designed to help you define leadership and to explore these questions.

Activities:

- A Picture is Worth a Thousand Words
- Dressed to Lead
- Instigator
- Team tag

A Picture is Worth a Thousand Words

Estimated Time

45 minutes

Tip:

Be sure you use books that have artwork that reflects the culture of your students.

Description:

This team activity explores the role of leadership in a team.

Learning Themes:

- Identify the effects of leadership on teamwork and team members.
- Demonstrate teamwork skills in activities.
- Exhibit an ability to collaborate as part of a team including leading and following.

Props:

- A variety of reproductions of art work (could be magazine cut outs, catalogs, postcards etc.) enough for each group of three to have one
- A pen/pencil and piece of paper for each student

Setup:

Create workspaces where students can spread out materials and work in teams of three.

Framing:

"Art can inspire us. What types of art inspire you? Images strike people in different ways. Let's see if we can work as a team to convey the story that we see in a picture."

Tip:

Switch it up! If your group is too energetic for a quiet activity, play tag and conversely, if your group is too tired for tag, do something quiet.

Procedure:

1. Have your group form teams of three.
2. Give each team a selection of art pieces, a large piece of paper and pens for everyone.
3. Ask them to select a picture that inspires them.
4. They will write a story inspired by the picture they selected. The story should relate to the concept of leadership.
5. Remind them that they are creating one story per team of three. Give them an appropriate time limit based on their ability to complete a task. Approximately 15 minutes.

Reflection:

Reflection Activity:

Have each team read their story and show the picture that inspired them to think about leadership. They should describe the inspiration.

Questions for Discussion:

1. How did you work as a team to write your story? (For example: Did one student transcribe while another wrote or did they each write a part, etc.?)

2. What do you think your major contribution to your team was?

3. What skill do you think you need to work on so that you can contribute more effectively to your team?

4. Who took a leadership role in your group? What did it look like and sound like?

5. Are there any skills your team members need to work on to become more active leaders? Can you give them feedback on that?

Dressed To Lead

Description:

Teams of students explore the characteristics of leadership through creativity.

Learning Themes:

- Identify the characteristics of leadership and teamwork.
- Exhibit an ability to collaborate as part of a team including leading and following.

Props:

- Art materials – enough for everyone to do collage and picture making
- Pieces of large paper – enough for everyone to have one
- Paper fasteners – five for each group
- Hole punch – one per group or you can simply share
- Examples of leadership costumes from magazines, history books etc.

Estimated Time

45 minutes

Setup:

Create workspaces where students can spread out materials and work in teams of three. Consider having examples for students to look at of positive leaders in a variety of costumes or dress (tribal leader, head coach, military leader, football quarterback, school principal, president, lead singer of a music group or band etc.). Choose a variety of roles, ethnicities and genders that will be familiar yet challenge students' thinking.

Framing:
"We all know how we like our leaders to act. If you don't know off the top of your head, just think about it. You have leaders in your family, right? Often this is mom and/or dad. How do like to be treated by the leader of your family? What is important for the leader of your family to do? Today we are going to work in teams to create costumes that positive leaders might wear."

Procedure:
1. Separate your group into teams of four students.
2. Give each team five to ten minutes to discuss the qualities they believe a leader should and does possess.
3. Have each member of the team decide on which body part, 1) head, 2) torso, 3) legs and 4) arms, of their leader they will represent. (If your group numbers are such that you have some groups of five, people can share a body part.)
4. "So your team has decided on the qualities your leader will possess. Keeping that in mind, what type of costume would you put on that body part?"
5. Have teams scatter so that one member can't see the others' work.
6. Give them 15-20 minutes to work on their body parts. Remind them to be as creative as they'd like.
7. Finally have teams come back together and assemble their leaders using the hole punch and paper fasteners. Have them discuss how they think their art work reflects the characteristics they talked about earlier. They should also identify some people who have leadership qualities. They should be prepared to talk about this with the group. Give them as much time as they need.

Reflection:
Reflection Activity:
1. Ask each team to share their creation and describe the qualities that they thought were important.
2. Have the presenter describe their creation.
3. What qualities are included in the costume?
4. Encourage conversation and dialogue about leadership qualities and what they look like in the students' worlds?
5. Are there any specific leaders you had in mind or used as reference when you created the various aspects of your leaders?

Instigator

Description:

This activity allows students to move as they experience the effects of being a leader and a follower.

Learning Themes:

- Exhibit an ability to collaborate as part of a team including leading and following.
- Understand what it is to focus on/pay attention to another.
- Analyze potential consequences of following others.

Props:

None

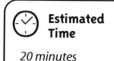

Estimated Time

20 minutes

Setup:

Select two students to be the "Detectives."

Framing:

"This activity gives you another chance to practice observation and leadership skills, while also seeing how one student's behavior can affect the rest of the group."

Tip:

Does your group just need some fun? Skip the framing, just give the rules and reflect on what happened regarding your FVC.

Procedure:

1. After the rules are explained, the Detectives are to leave the room.

2. Once the two Detective students have left the room, designate one of the remaining students to be the "Instigator" (leader). This student will be the leader whom the rest of the group will have to follow.

3. Instruct students to follow the lead of the designated Instigator/leader. Whatever the Instigator/leader does, they are to copy.

4. The Instigator/leader will make different movements, gestures, etc., as he or she moves around the room (e.g., snapping fingers, hopping on one foot, skipping, etc).

5. The activity begins when the two Detectives are invited back into the room.

6. As the group moves around the room, the Detectives try to guess who is leading the rest of the group in their movements.

7. Give the Detectives three opportunities to guess who the Instigator/leader is.

8. Select two new Detectives and play again.

Reflection:

1. Which did you enjoy more – being an Instigator/leader or a Detective?

2. Instigators/leaders, were you trying to be sneaky or did you not care if the Detectives found you out?

3. For followers, were you trying to pretend you were the Instigator/leader?

4. How did the Detectives do their work?

5. Why are observation skills important to leadership?

 Additional Thoughts

• *Give as many people as you can a chance to be the Detectives and Instigators.*

• *Try to promote a conversation about how leaders can instigate people to act positively or negatively and relate to specifics in your program environment.*

Team Tag

Estimated Time

20 minutes

Description:
Using vigorous physical activity, students explore the roles of leadership and followership.

Learning Themes:
- Identify the characteristics of leadership and teamwork.
- Learn to work together to achieve a common goal or task.
- Exhibit an ability to collaborate as part of a team including leading and following.

Props:
- A different colored fleece ball for each team

Setup:
Use an obstacle-free space such as half of a basketball court or field with defined boundaries.

Framing:
"It is important to have leaders who see the big picture. When we are focused on the small tasks that we need to do, we need leaders to help us see the big picture."

Procedure:

1. Ask students to form small groups of four to five players.

2. Give each small group a differently colored fleece ball.

3. Explain to the group that they can tag anyone but their own teammates.

4. In this version, if someone gets tagged, they stop wherever they are but can get back into the game if the "re-play" object is tossed to them. The "re-play" object is the fleece ball each team has. Each team should have a ball that is a different color from the other teams.

5. If a player with the "re-play" object is tagged, he or she needs to toss it to another player on their team and then have it tossed back to return to the game.

6. Players are not allowed to interfere with other teams' "re-play" objects.

7. When the game is over, after a minute or two, the team with the most players still moving gains a point.

8. Play several rounds allowing a short planning time in between.

9. Have teams keep track of how many points they have.

Reflection:

1. Did you switch between being a leader and a follower in this activity? If so, can you explain that to us?

2. Tell me about some of your favorite leaders. Who do you think helped them by working hard, maybe behind the scenes or on the details/little picture that others might not have seen? (Use an example that works for you like… "One of my favorite leaders is Martin Luther King Jr. and he always said he couldn't have accomplished so much without the help of his wife Coretta.") Did you see anyone play that role in this activity?

3. Ask students to fill in the blank: "If I were the leader for a day I would ………"

 Tip:

As a reflection piece, have students write out #3 in such a way that their responses can be posted and displayed in classroom.)

Section II: Responsible Decision Making

Being a positive leader and a good follower involves responsible decision making. Responsible decision making, according to CASEL is, "making decisions based on accurate consideration of all relevant factors and the likely consequences of alternative courses of actions, respecting others and taking responsibility for one's decisions." Further support for the need to develop responsible decision-making skills is included in The Search Institute's 40 Developmental Assets for Adolescents™. These decision-making skills are also highly significant in promoting resiliency and positive youth development. Clearly an ability to make and follow through on good decisions is fundamental to living a healthy life and being a positive leader. Unfortunately, many of our students have not developed the competency in this area and that is what has brought them to our programs. The utilization of the following activities will help you to not only initiate conversations regarding decision making but will also give students an opportunity to practice and develop these skills.

In addition to the reflection questions at the end of each activity, you may find the following questions helpful in further exploring the topic of decision making:

- What is the difference between passive and active decision making?
- What do I do when making an active decision and can I recognize it?
- What influences my ability to make a good decision?
- How can I solve problems that arise and what are my resources?
- What are some of the consequences of decisions I have made? Both responsible and irresponsible decisions?
- Am I likely to go along, without thinking about my actions when I am with a group of friends?
- Can I see how a decision (group or individual) changed the outcome of an activity?
- Can I see how environmental or social factors may influence my ability to make good decisions?
- Can I see how my decisions affect others?

Activities:
- 4 Quad
- Decision Dilemma
- The Rope Push
- The Rules of the Game

4 Quad

Description:
This dynamic group activity explores goal setting and how decisions are made to attain those goals.

Learning Themes:
- Display an ability to make decisions that support community norms and pro-social behaviors.
- Describe or demonstrate the benefits of positive and challenging goals.
- Demonstrate an ability to ask questions, negotiate, and support team decisions.

Props:
- 2 20 ft. lengths of accessory rope or cord (align with what is in pack bag)
- 2 balls per student

Estimated Time

35 minutes

Tip:

Consider asking the group to identify a leader for this activity.

Setup:
- Ask two students to hold a 20 ft. length of accessory cord at shoulder height and keep it taut. Then ask two more students to do the same, standing so that their cord is perpendicular to the first cord. This will form a four square area.
- Distribute balls of four distinct colors to the group, asking students to take two balls each. (The color that each person grabs is irrelevant at this time.) Once everyone has their balls, they are to separate into four even groups, each group standing in one quadrant of the four-quad area.

Framing:
"As you perform this activity, think about how you are working as a team. You have two tasks to accomplish together. First, separate all of the balls by color into each of the four quadrants. Second, after the balls are separated, the groups who are opposite each other must exchange balls. Here are the rules…"

Procedure:
1. Ask students to set a group goal for how many balls they can exchange in two minutes.
2. All balls must be tossed; there can be no hand-to-hand exchanges.
3. Pretend that the grid is a wall that runs up to the sky and down to the ground and cannot be penetrated by anything but the balls.
4. Balls cannot be passed or tossed under a cord; they must go over the cord.

5. Balls can be held only in people's hands and never tucked in clothing or stored between one's arm and side, for example.

6. Penalties:

   a. Five seconds less play time for any dropped ball. A dropped ball remains out of play once it is dropped.

   b. Ten seconds less play time for touching the cord itself.

7. Give the students four attempts at this activity. Round one will be their first goal-setting attempt and will determine their baseline number of balls. Future goals should be set based on this information.

Reflection:

1. How did the group come to agreement on the goal you set?

2. What was effective or positive about this decision-making process?

3. How did you make decisions? Was there consensus? Did you push each other? Did anyone feel pushed into making a decision he or she wasn't comfortable with?

4. Who showed leadership skills in this activity?

5. Did they encourage the making of responsible decisions and goals?

6. Raise your hand if you think you were both a leader and a follower at different times during this activity. Ask for examples of both leadership and followership.

7. At times in life, we are all leaders. What are some responsible decisions you have made in your life?

Reflection Activity:

1. One way we understand that leaders are making responsible decisions is by their words and statements. Ask your students to write bumper stickers that capture statements that leaders might make to communicate responsible decision making that supports their followers. The bumper sticker might read, "I've got your back" or "I'm here for you."

   "We can make it happen," "Yes, we can," "We can make a difference."

> **Tip:**
>
> *Students should be stating their own and others' skills within these answers. In this way, they will be demonstrating awareness of and appreciation for self and others.*

Decision Dilemma

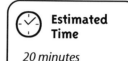

Estimated Time

20 minutes

Description:

This activity explores the process of making and following through on a good decision.

Learning Themes:

- Demonstrate responsible and healthy decision making.
- Solve problems by analyzing causes and potential solutions.
- Describe what constitutes a healthy choice.
- Display an ability to make decisions that support community norms and pro-social behaviors.

Props:

- Tossables, at least one per student
- Masking Tape
- Markers

Setup:

You will need a small, open play space for this activity.

Framing (Part 1):

"Sometimes we make good decisions, sometimes we make bad ones. All of us do. How do we know we've made a good or bad decision because they all seem good or at least fun when we make them?" Give your students time to answer. You're looking for the outcome or what happens next. If needed, prod with, "The other day I drove by a Dairy Queen and the poster of that sundae looked too good to pass up. It sure tasted good, but I am trying to lose weight." (This is just a suggestion – use an authentic example; you may be thin or the nearest Dairy Queen may be 30 miles away.) Do you think that was a good or bad decision? Why?'"

Procedure (Part 1):

1. Ask your students to form a circle.
2. Ask them to think of some healthy or positive decisions. Then, discuss what the positive outcomes were. Have your students discuss them and challenge inappropriate outcomes. (Flip chart the healthy/positive choices that students identified. Keep them posted)
3. Ask each student to pick one outcome. Give them a piece of masking tape and a marker and have them write their chosen outcome on their piece of tape.
4. Hand each student a tossable and have them stick their tape on it.

Framing (Part 2):

"Now we have all these healthy outcomes. Let's see what can happen when you try to make lots of healthy things happen at once."

Procedure (Part 2):

1. Have students remain in their circle and ask for a volunteer to come into the middle. This person is the decider.

2. Explain that the decider yells, "One, two, three, Go." On "Go" all the students throw their 'outcomes' in the air in the direction of the decider.

3. The decider tries to catch as many outcomes as he or she can. He or she should then read the 'caught' outcomes out loud followed by the outcomes that he or she missed.

4. Give everyone who wants one a turn in the middle.

Reflection:

1. Did anyone not catch an outcome at all? Why do you think that was?

2. Did anyone miss the outcome they really wanted? Why do you think that was?

3. What do you think would have happened if you'd just paid attention to the outcome you really wanted?

4. What steps are involved in making decisions that help you to achieve desired positive outcomes?

Tip:

If you have done the Goal Mapping activity, use those worksheets as fodder for your reflection.

Variations

• *For large groups: have two or more students in the middle.*

• *For small groups or if one or more of your students wants an added challenge: make your circle wider so thrown tossables aren't too close together.*

The Rope Push

Description:

This fun activity explores how we make decisions, sometimes without thinking as much as we should.

Learning Themes:

- Analyze potential consequences of following others.
- Identify methods used to recognize and avoid threatening situations.
- Implement decision-making skills, refusal skills and goal setting to avoid risky situations.
- Solve problems by analyzing causes and potential solutions.

Props:

- A 60-80 ft. length of game rope
- Masking tape
- 4 cones, 2 medium lengths of rope, etc. as boundary markers

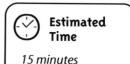

Estimated Time

15 minutes

Setup:

1. Lay rope on the ground and mark the middle with masking tape.
2. Give each team a boundary that is approximately one foot from the middle of the rope so there will be about a two foot area in which students aren't allowed.

Framing:

"Sometimes we get so caught up in doing something and we keep having the same outcomes. We don't even think about doing it another way – it's just the way we always did it. We're stuck!"

Procedure:

1. Divide the group in half and position each team behind their boundary.
2. Explain that they will have three minutes to get as much of their rope into the area of the other team.
3. No going into the two-foot no man's zone
4. No going into the other team's area
5. No pulling the rope
6. The winner will be hard to judge.
7. Play a couple of rounds without planning and a couple with planning.

Reflection:

1. Did anyone win?
2. Was there anyone really caught up in trying to beat the other team?
3. If so, were you focused on where to put the rope or on winning?
4. Was there anyone who was just doing what everyone else was doing?
5. When are times that you choose to follow others?
6. What are some of the outcomes of that behavior?
7. I sometimes realize I'm making a decision without considering what it means because I am just doing it the way I always do it or the way my friends do it. Does that ever happen to you? Does anything change once you recognize that behavior?

The Rules of the Game

Estimated Time

20 minutes

Tip:

Use this activity to reinforce some of the concepts covered in other areas of this guide, i.e., Full Value Contract words.

Description:

This activity explores how differing goals can make people feel and behave differently.

Learning Themes:

- Demonstrate an ability to evaluate and revise personal and/or group goals.
- Describe how one's choices and decisions impact the achievement of goals.
- Support each other in achieving goals and making decisions.

Props:

- 5 Hula™ type hoops
- 30 or more small balls (tennis or fleece)
- Masking tape
- Markers
- A game rope, cones or other boundary markers

Setup:

1. Label each ball with a letter as in Scrabble™, but skip some of the really hard letters like Q, Z, or X. So you might have: 4 Es, 3 As, 3 Is, 2 Os, 2 Ns, 2 Rs, 3 Ts, 1 L, 2 Ss, 1 U, 2 Ds, 1 G, 1 B, 1 C, 1 M, 1 P, 1 F, 1 H and 1 Y. This combination will yield thirty-one letters.

2. Set up the hoops with one in the middle and the remaining four on the outside forming a square. This formation will look like the five on a die. Place the hoops further apart to enable more running

3. Designate a home area for each team, using game rope or the like, inside which the team and their hoop can fit.

4. Put all the labeled balls in the middle hoop.

Framing:

"Sometimes we are all working toward the same goal. Let's see how things change when our goals change. I bet our roles and the decisions we make will change as our goals change."

Procedure:

1. Divide your students into four small groups.

2. Each small group should circle up in and around one hoop.

3. On "Go," one student will run to the middle and get one ball/letter and place it in his or her home hoop. Once the ball/letter is in the hoop and the returning student has high-fived another member of his or her team, another student can leave to get another letter.

4. Only one student at a time may be out of the home area getting a letter. All students should go at least once before a student goes twice.

5. Students may get letters from another team's hoop. Students may not defend their hoop.

6. The goal is for them to get letters to spell a five-letter word. The team can have more than five balls in their hoop.

7. Give your students time to plan before commencing each round.

ROUND TWO

8. The same rules apply. But you will whisper, or say in a way that the other groups can't overhear, a new goal for each team. New goals are:
   - Team 1: Get five vowels.
   - Team 2: Get five consonants.
   - Team 3: Get five letters in alphabetical sequence (i.e.: a, b, c, d, e).
   - Team 4: Spell a five letter word again.

9. Give your students time to plan.

10. Stop the action at random times to ask students to make observations about how they are working together.

Reflection:

1. When all four teams had the same goal, did you really have the same goal?

2. Did your team have a strategy?

3. How did you make decisions that helped you to achieve your goals and implement your strategy?

4. What decisions would you change? (Go to other team's hoop instead of the middle to get balls?)

5. How did you contribute to your team's decision-making process? (Go around the group and ask your students to give examples of their own and others' helpfulness. You should also give examples.)

6. When it came time to execute your strategy, how did you decide who would do what? Or, was your strategy developed by what you felt your team members were good at? (For example, "Jessica is a really fast runner. If she were on my team, I would have suggested she get all the letters.")

7. In our classroom, are there goals or areas where we could be making better decisions?

Variations

• *Everyone has to get at least one letter.*

• *Have your students spell specific words. Adjust your balls/letters to what is needed to make those words. Don't make it too easy!*

Section III: Social Awareness — Empathy

Mary Gordon, author of *Roots of Empathy: Changing the World Child by Child* and renowned Canadian social entrepreneur, said in an interview with Amy Eldon for PBS's GlobalTribe: "Once children are of school age, the single most important thing we can do to advance pro-social behavior… is to foster empathy."[16] Empathy is not only important to the development of leadership skills among at-risk children and youth, it is fundamental to all social functioning. Trying to help someone develop social awareness is a bit tricky. Our work has shown us that we need to provide an environment where it is safe to explore our beliefs – the beliefs that we have about ourselves and others – and do so in a way in which feedback is constructive and caring. This process and the resulting expression of thoughts, beliefs and feelings is what will help your students develop competency in the art of Empathy. The following activities are a step in this direction.

Activities:

- Boop
- Everybody Up
- Jedi Knights
- Kind Words
- Swat Tag
- Tag with Hecklers
- Tin Shoe

---

16. http://www.pbs.org/kcet/globaltribe/voices/voi_gordon.html#top

Boop

Estimated Time

10 minutes

Description:

This lively activity explores how people can help one another.

Learning Themes:

- Understand and describe healthy relationships.
- Know and appreciate one's peers.
- Define and identify ways of caring for and helping self and others.

Props:

- Two to five blown up balloons – enough for teams of three to four to have one (and maybe a spare or two for popping)

Setup:

Identify an obstacle-free play environment.

Framing:

"Your balloon represents the spirits and feelings of another group member who is feeling down about him or herself. His or her tendency is to sink down to the floor because he or she is so overwhelmed. Your task is to work together to lift the spirits of this person, and keep them up."

Tip:

Remember students can be connected by holding a piece of rope or a bandanna rather than each other's hands.

Procedure:

1. Separate your group into teams of three to four.
2. Teams should hold hands to form circles – make sure there is enough room between teams to move.
3. Give each team a balloon and time to practice keeping it off the ground while holding hands. They need to hold hands throughout the game.
4. Now call out a body part "Feet" for example. That is the body part they need to use to keep the balloon up.
5. Switch body parts every 10 to 15 seconds. Move from easy (hands) to hard (nose, for example).
6. Now call out combinations, like hand, elbow and knee. This means a hit with a hand needs to be followed by one with an elbow and then a knee.
7. You can do the final round with "No body parts at all." It can be done – blowing is one way.

Reflection:

1. Did it work, could you help keep someone's spirits up? If so, how did you do it?

2. Do you think you can always help someone or do you think there will be/are times when you can't? If so, when?

3. How did you discover a way to work together? Did you make a plan?

4. What was it like to work together with different parts of your body? Could you sense what the next move would be?

5. Did you notice anyone having a hard time or struggling? Did you help them?

6. What are some ways you can develop healthy relationships with others?

7. Did anyone have any physical problems they had to consider while doing this activity?

Everybody Up

Description:

Students will use their strength to explore the concept of supporting one another in this activity.

Learning Themes:

- Understand and describe healthy relationships.
- Define and identify ways of caring for and helping self and others.
- Demonstrate an ability to appropriately express one's needs and emotions.

Props:

I Am About Cards*

Estimated Time

15 minutes

Setup:

Create a space that is obstacle free and has room for movement. Make sure that there is obstacle-free space behind students while they are attempting this activity.

Framing

"Being a responsible friend involves supporting but not overpowering another person. Let's practice those skills with each other."

---

* Available from Project Adventure

Procedure:

1. Have students find partners. It is helpful (easier), but not necessary if they team up with someone close to their size.

2. Ask two students to sit on the floor facing one another. Their toes should be touching, their knees bent, and their bottoms on the floor.

3. Explain that the goal of the activity is for each pair to simultaneously help each other to stand.

4. Give the pairs a couple of opportunities to practice and be successful, and then ask the pairs to team with other pairs and attempt the same process with four people.

5. Continue to join with other pairs until eventually the whole group is making the attempt together.

Reflection:

1. How were you able to stand together with one other person (two other people, and so on)?

2. What did you have to understand about what the other person needed to make the activity successful for you?

3. Did everyone get what they needed to make it work for them? What were some of those needs?

4. Did you talk to each other to find out each others' needs or did you just know? What were some offers that people made to provide help?

5. When you are trying to help someone, do you think it is better to ask them what they need or try to figure it out yourself?

Reflection Activity:

1. Using the I am About Cards, ask your students to find images that represent help.

2. Then, ask them to describe ways they think the people whose images are on the cards may have helped each other.

Jedi Knights

Description:

Students will participate in vigorous physical activity to explore the roles of leaders and how they determine when others need help.

Learning Themes:

- Identify the characteristics of leadership and teamwork.
- Demonstrate social awareness through empathic and caring statements and/or behavior.
- Demonstrate self awareness through the expression of thoughts and feelings.

Props:

- 2 foam noodles
- 2 spot markers
- 1 fleece ball for each student
- A game rope

 Estimated Time

30 minutes

Tip:

Always make framing and reflection relevant. This activity uses a Star Wars theme; if that is not appropriate for your group for cultural or other reasons, use something more suitable.

Setup:

- Create two teams and position them about three to five feet from a line that your game rope creates between them.
- Hand out one fleece ball per student. Place them all on the line.
- Also give each team a spot marker and a noodle for their Jedi Knight.

Framing:

Each team will designate one Jedi Knight. The Jedi Knight is your leader who you will be trying to protect and who, in turn, can save you."

Procedure:

1. Instruct each team to position their Jedi Knight in a way that they can most easily protect him or her. The Jedi Knight stands on the spot marker and holds a noodle.
2. One team is given all of the fleece balls.
3. At "Go" the team with the balls throws them at the opposite team. All throws need to be below the shoulders.
4. If hit by a ball, the student crouches down in the spot where he or she was struck. If the student was holding a ball when hit, he or she releases it so that a teammate can pick it up. The student who was hit can only be freed by the Jedi Knight.

5. Students who are not hit with a fleece ball can retrieve the balls and toss them back, trying to tag the other team.

6. The Jedi Knight, at any time, can leave his or her spot marker and free teammates by tagging them with the noodle. Once revived by the light saber, the individual can resume play.

7. The Jedi Knight is safe when he or she is on the spot marker – being hit by the ball doesn't bother him or her

8. If the Jedi Knight is hit with a ball when off the spot marker, the round is over. All balls are returned to the dividing line. All balls are given to the opposite team, everyone is freed and the second round begins.

Reflection:

1. Did the Knights help the teams and, if so, how?

2. If you were a Jedi, how did it feel to be protected (when on spot maker), but really vulnerable when you were freeing others?

3. If you were a Jedi, what did you feel your responsibilities to your followers were?

4. If you were a follower, what do you think your responsibilities to your Knight were?

5. If the Jedi was a leader, what did you think he or she was feeling? And what did you feel as a follower?

Reflection Activity:

1. List the leadership qualities that were demonstrated on flip chart paper.

2. List the feelings that leaders had.

3. List the feelings that followers had.

4. Then ask them to write in their journal about the leadership and followership feelings that they experienced today.

Variation

• *Instead of giving one team or the other all the balls to begin the round, place the balls on the dividing line. At "Go" all the followers try to get as many balls as they can for their team. From there, play proceeds as described.*

Kind Words

Estimated Time

30 minutes

Description:
This activity helps students define empathy.

Learning Themes:
- Demonstrate social awareness through empathic and caring statements and/or behavior.
- Demonstrate self awareness through the expression of thoughts and feelings.
- Increase one's emotional vocabulary.

Props:
- One index/note card with a letter written on it per student (see Setup)

Setup:
- Choose some words that define empathy to you, e.g.:

  Understand

  Give

  Aware

  Compassion

  Sensitive

  Share

  Etc. (words should be ones that your students will understand)
- Write one letter for each word you've chosen on an index card so that a set of index cards spells the words you have identified that define empathy, i.e., SHARE would have five index cards: S, H, A, R, and E; COMPASSION would add C, (2)O, M, P, S, I, and N. They would already have an A and S from SHARE.
- If you need more cards to ensure that each student gets one, make a couple with * on them. These will be wild cards and can represent any letter they want or need.

Framing:
"In order to lead people, we need to understand them – what they are feeling – and people need to be able to understand their leaders, right? A word that is used to describe that concept is empathy. Let's explore that word."

Procedure:

1. Explain to your students that you will be giving them enough letters to spell a word that defines empathy. They will each have one letter on cards you hand out, to spell _____ (however many words you have made letter cards for, as described in the Setup) words. Explain that you have also given out _____ wild cards (however many cards with * on them that you've given out).

2. Further explain that when you say: "Go," your students should find other students with letters to spell a word that means empathy. Remind them that you know they have the letters for _____ words, but you'd love to be surprised! Ask them to raise their hands when they have a word.

3. Shout, "Go!" Give them a minute or two.

4. Go around and have each group tell you their word. Let your students know when they have surprised you with a word you didn't think of.

5. Play new rounds by either challenging students to come up with new words from the cards they already have or giving them a new set of cards.

Reflection:

Reflection Activity:

1. Use the Pi Chart technique that you learned in a previous activity to define what the word empathy, looks like, sounds like and feels like.

Swat Tag

Description:

This quick activity gives students an opportunity to demonstrate and explain empathy.

Learning Themes:

- Define and identify ways of caring for and helping self and others.
- Demonstrate social awareness through empathic and caring statements and/or behavior.
- Demonstrate self awareness through the expression of thoughts and feelings.

Props:

- 1 foam noodle
- 1 Hula™ type hoop
- 1 spot marker per student

Estimated Time

15 minutes

Tip:

Don't let an unathletic student become trapped as the swatter. If you think you have such a student in your group, make it a rule that people can only be the swatter during three rounds.

Setup:

1. Ask the group to stand in a circle. Give each student a spot marker and ask them to stand on it.

2. Have one student, the swatter, stand in the middle of the circle with a noodle.

3. Finally, place a hoop in the middle of the circle.

Framing:

"This is a game of speed! How quickly can you flee and how quickly can you chase? Think about the role you and other people play in this game."

Procedure:

1. The swatter can move freely inside the circle while he or she chooses a peer to tag.

2. Tapping someone below the knee with the noodle constitutes a tag. Students should not try to avoid this tag.

3. Once a peer is tagged, the swatter races back to the hoop and drops (not throws) the noodle in the hoop. At the same time, the person tagged goes into the middle. (see safety note below to help avoid collisions).

4. Once the noodle lands on the ground, the tagged student picks it up and attempts to hit the swatter before he or she runs back to the spot vacated by the first student tagged.

5. If the swatter successfully makes it to the vacant spot in the circle, he or she remains there and the tagged person becomes the swatter.

6. If the original swatter gets tagged on the way to the vacant spot in the circle, he or she remains in the middle. That student remains the swatter until he or she successfully gets back to a spot marker.

Reflection:

1. What was the most fun for you – being swatted or being the swatter? Can you explain that?

2. Do different people in our group feel more comfortable in different roles?

3. Why do you think that is?

4. Do you think it helps our group to have people in it with different feelings? Why?

5. How do you think this activity connects to empathy / understanding another person's feelings or point of view?

6. In what ways did empathy show up in this activity?

7. What are some ways that we can help others in our program using empathy?

Variation

• *You may allow students, at anytime, to move to an empty spot. This means that the pair who is playing the original game may be locked out of the original spot that they are trying to return to! Anyone who chooses to move to an empty spot, however, can be tagged whenever they are not standing on a spot.*

Tag with Hecklers

Description:

This tag activity simulates the experience of name-calling so students can reflect on it as it relates to social and self awareness.

Learning Themes:

- Demonstrate social awareness through empathic and caring statements and/or behavior.
- Learn the subtle cues that people use to express their emotions.
- Demonstrate an ability to appropriately express one's needs and emotions.

Props:

- A game rope or other boundary marker(s)

Estimated Time

15 minutes

Setup:

Set a rope so that students can easily stand outside the perimeter of the rope, but the interior takes up as much space as possible within the room you have.

It is important to read through this and make sure your group is ready for the challenge.

Framing:

"This tag game is one in which you will experience being an outsider. Most of us have experienced this. Remember, this is just a game and we're doing these things so that we can talk about them."

Procedure:

1. This is basically any tag game you like played inside a boundary. You may want to play the first round while fast walking versus running. You could also start out with a small playing area then expand it each round.

2. Instead of becoming It, the person tagged goes outside the boundary and heckles the players by saying: "_____ (name of student) is goofy." Ask your students to think of a variety of ways they can say "goofy" with attitude. Let them know that they will be using the word 'goofy' as an example of name calling and it will be applied to everyone so please do not take it personally.

3. Remind the players not to pick on one student.

4. Play several rounds so that everyone experiences being the first one out and the last one standing.

Tip:

Feel free to change this to something nice (e.g., is kind, is fun, etc.). Or students could just make distracting noises.

Reflection:

1. What was it like to watch your friends heckle each other?
2. Show some body language of people heckling.
3. Show some body language of the students who were being heckled.
4. How did you feel in this activity?
5. How do you think others felt when being called names?
6. Could you tell when others were being serious with their put down/put ups? How did you know this? What were you looking for?
7. How can we help each other to use more put ups than put downs?

Tin Shoe

Estimated Time

30 minutes

Description:

This activity enables students to give and receive appreciative feedback.

Learning Themes:

- Support each other in achieving goals and making decisions.
- Exhibit an ability to accept, acknowledge and appreciate differences.
- Demonstrate self awareness through the expression of thoughts and feelings.
- Demonstrate social awareness through empathic and caring statements and/or behavior.

Props:

- Two large tin cans (the kind used in the school cafeteria filled with canned vegetables or the like)
- Two fleece balls per student
- Masking tape
- Markers
- A note card for each student

Setup:

1. Write one student's name on each of the note/index cards before you hand them out.
2. Ask your students to sit on the floor in a circle.

Framing:
"We all have good qualities; ways we act that help us and help others. These are not external qualities like how we look and what we wear, but how we act/how we behave. Take a minute to think about qualities you and others have such as cooperating, sharing and supporting others. Keep these thoughts to yourself for right now."

Procedure:
1. Give each student an index/note card, making sure they don't get their own name. Ask them not to share the name you've given them with other students.

2. Give each student two fleece balls, two pieces of tape (not long, just enough so they can write a name and a quality on each) and a marker.

3. Ask them to write the name on their index card and a quality that person has on one piece of tape. They should then stick this onto one of their fleece balls. Remind them that they should be positive and refer not to how people look, but how they act. For example, being friendly works, having a cool haircut doesn't work. Also ask them to think of an example of this person using this quality. It should be something they will be comfortable talking about.

4. Then ask them to write a quality they have and their name on another fleece ball. Again this quality should be something they will be comfortable sharing.

5. Circulate one can and have your students put their qualities inside it. Then circulate the other can and have your students put the qualities for their peers in it.

6. Tell them that now their challenge is to take care of those qualities by not spilling them while they send the cans around the circle using only their feet. Ask them to set a goal for how long it will take to pass them along.

7. Let them do a trial run before setting their goal so they can make an attainable goal.

8. Time them as they pass the cans. They can choose to pass them in the same direction for an easier challenge or in opposite directions for a harder challenge. Give them a five-second penalty each time they spill the can.

9. Do further rounds as you and they see fit.

Reflection:
Reflection Activity:
1. Pull the balls out of each can one at a time. Discuss each quality as you pull it out.

2. For the balls with peer qualities on them, find out who wrote them. Ask that student to share why he or she wrote this quality for his or her peer and to give an example of this quality. Then ask the whole group if there is another quality this person has that they might add to the first quality and/or do they have further examples of this quality used by the student in question.

3. For the balls on which they wrote their own qualities, ask each student why they wrote that quality and compare them to the qualities their peers wrote and talked about. Point it out gently if someone over or under stated his or her qualities.

4. Finish by making sure the air is clear by asking: "Does anyone need to discuss anything that happened?"

Appendix

Adventure as a Tool for Behavior Management

Project Adventure's Behavior Management through Adventure (BMTA) is a researched model that provides training and an operational plan for schools, agencies and organizations to create a healthy environment. An environment in which children and youth can:

- Increase social and emotional competency.
- Increase academic success.
- Become responsible for their goals and decisions.
- Practice and begin to replicate new behaviors and skills.

BMTA provides real tools and strategies that, when appropriately applied, facilitate an effective change in the way staff interact with children, youth and their colleagues. Through the application of meta-cognition to social emotional learning, BMTA is not only a behavior management model, but is also a methodology that improves long-term outcomes. The power of BMTA is that children and youth are guided through a process in which they take responsibility for and develop the therapeutic/learning environment. BMTA is currently being applied in a wide variety of settings from alternative schools to juvenile justice to residential programs.

BMTA Development

BMTA was developed by Project Adventure Inc. (PA) as an outcome of Adventure Based Counseling. In 1980, Project Adventure established a direct service program in Covington, GA under the leadership of Cindy Simpson. PA's Adventure Based Counseling program evolved into a holistic approach that has flourished throughout the entire PA Georgia milieu – and is in constant use: in the classroom, during recreation time, during free time and in the residences. PA's Full Value Contract has become the language for discussing behaviors and goals and the Adventure Group Process has become the tool for reflection, growth and change. With a range of programs, Project Adventure's Georgia Campus, now known as Project Adventure Kids (www.projectadventurekids.org), has been a restraint-free environment since its inception. It has maintained significant evidence of low recidivism and success for youth and children.

In the late 1990s, schools and agencies began to look to Project Adventure to learn how to replicate our restraint-free environment for students in therapeutic placements. This is when we refined our methodology into a replicable model that provides intense staff development and consultation. This model that has been successfully implemented in alternative schools, juvenile justice schools and residential and community based programs.

Some of the results PA has accumulated for its BMTA programs in Georgia are included here. Our most notable results have been in the area of recidivism. The following data were collected by Georgia's Department of Juvenile Justice:

- From 1991 to 2001, Choices (a 16+ week program for adjudicated youth involved with substance abuse) graduates were returned to detention at a rate of 15.53%.

- From 1991 to 2001, Challenge (an 8 to 12 week program for adjudicated youth) graduates were returned to detention at a rate of 29.06%.

- From 1996 to 2001, Legacy (a 1+ year program for adjudicated youth convicted of sexual abuse) graduates since 1996 were returned at a rate of 6.75% (Legacy graduated its first client in 1996.)

- Independent Living (a long-term program for graduates of interventions who are homeless and/or victims of abuse and neglect) graduates since 1998 (IL graduated its first client in 1998) returned to detention at only an 8% rate.

PA performed an internal evaluation of Project Decision, a non-residential alternative to out-of-school suspension for a school system local to its GA office. This evaluation found that during the first year and one half of the program a comparison of disciplinary incidents prior to and after attendance during the semester in which they were suspended had a statistically significant drop.

In October 2004, Project Adventure began to work with two public schools in Lawrence, Massachusetts to train and support their staff in the use of the BMTA program model. This is one of several schools, youth service agencies, and residential programs that have contracted with Project Adventure for BMTA training.

Lawrence is a high-need, urban community. Its public schools serve about 12,000 students. The vast majority of students are Hispanic (87%), speak a first language other than English (83%), and come from low-income families (83%). The district's most recent four-year graduation rate was 41% – lowest among all districts in the state. The two schools involved in implementing the BMTA program (one an elementary/middle school and the other a high school) both serve special education students referred from across the district.

Project Adventure worked with staff from the elementary/middle school to conduct a preliminary assessment of the impact of the BMTA program on both student and organizational outcomes. The assessment relied exclusively on data gathered by the schools or the district for its own purposes or for reporting to the Massachusetts Department of Education. Using baseline data, the assessment revealed a substantial decline in the use of physical restraints by staff with students, greater use of in-school suspensions rather than out-of-school suspensions, increased time on task (based on direct classroom observation), and improved teacher attendance. Participating students demonstrated improved attendance relative to all students in the district and the state, improved performance on the statewide academic assessment tests relative to all students in the district and all special needs students in the state, and improved performance on a commercial standardized academic assessment (Measures of Academic Progress) administered by the district.

Assessment of another BMTA Implementation at Stillwater Residential Treatment Facility (RTF), Chenango Forks, NY revealed the following:

As a result of the training and technical assistance provided by Project Adventure and the commitment of Stillwater RTF leadership and staff, the BMTA model has become an integral component of the daily operation and overall function of Stillwater RTF. Although the implementation process remains a "work in progress," substantial gains have been made in staff use of all five BMTA program components, including the Full Value Contract, student empowerment, group process, goal-setting, and adventure-based activities.. Our interviews with RTF staff have documented a range of structural changes that both demonstrate and support this result. In addition, students have embraced the components of BMTA with enthusiasm – regularly citing the Full Value Contract, Calling Group, and engaging in adventure activities.

> *"At first [staff] never thought that [BMTA] would take hold, and it seemed like things wouldn't change. But, after a few months of learning the model through trainings and practice, it became second nature."*

Impact of BMTA implementation on the use of restraints was almost immediate. The use of restraints with residents declined substantially within the first few months of BMTA implementation as staff were provided with effective alternatives. Of equal significance, this decline in restraint use has been sustained over the last two years despite continuing turnover among both staff and residents.

In the two years prior to the implementation of the BMTA model (2004 to 2006), staff generally conducted from 15 to 30 restraints each month – with peaks of 38 in May 2006 and 34 in November 2006. In the last quarter of 2006 (as BMTA training began), Stillwater averaged 27 restraints per month. During the first quarter of 2007 (as BMTA implementation began), the average monthly restraint rate declined to 17. During April 2007, there were only 4 restraints. Over the next 18 months, the rate of restraints remained at this lower level. During this period, there were ten months with five restraints or less. During one month, there were no restraints. Only twice did the number of restraints in a month exceed 10.

Activity Guide Worksheets

Goal Mapping

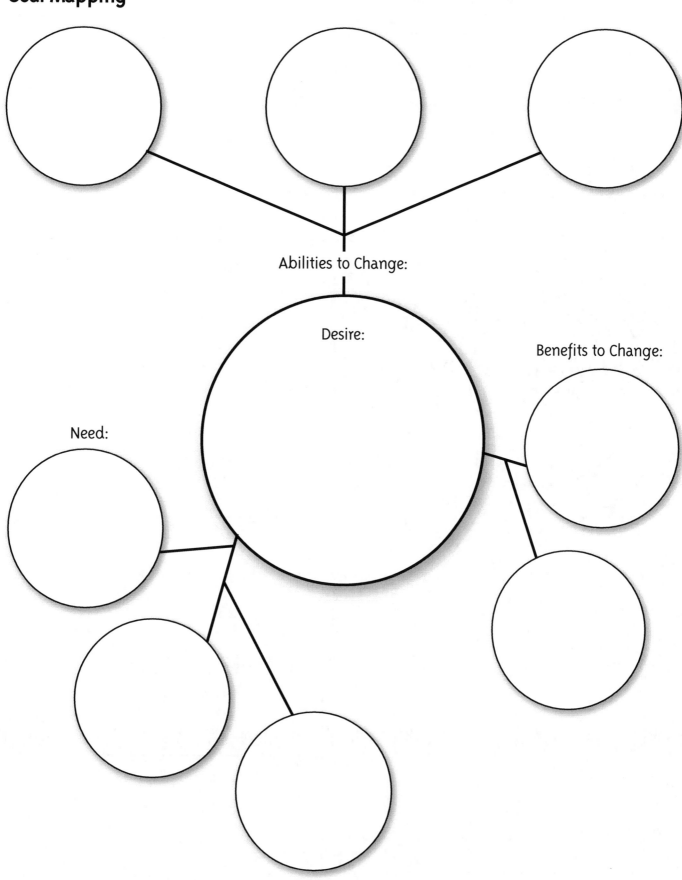

Abilities to Change:

Desire:

Benefits to Change:

Need:

Target Practice

I will (What is the goal I want to accomplish?) _____

_____

_____

Why is this goal important to me? _____

_____

_____

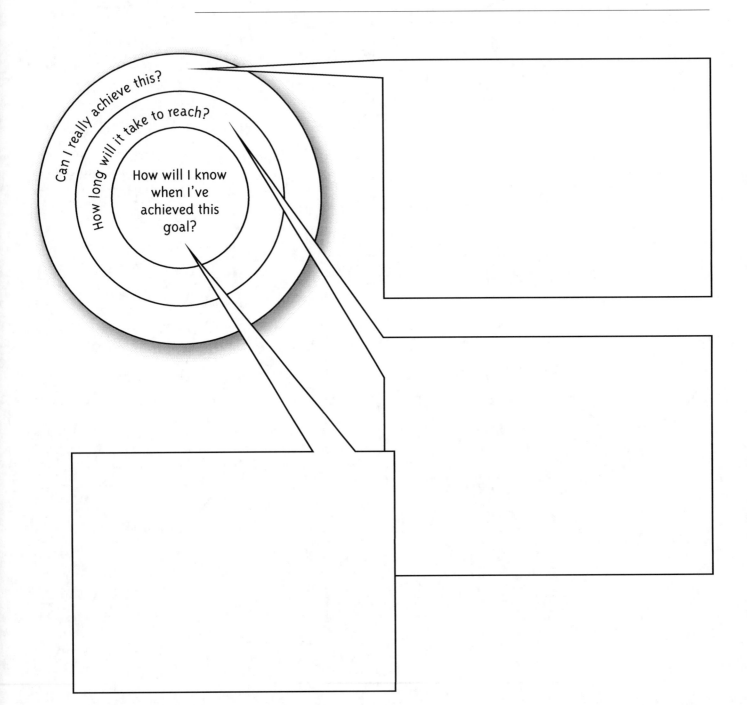

Rules? What Rules?

1. Write your ideas of what each Full Value means to you in each section of the pie.

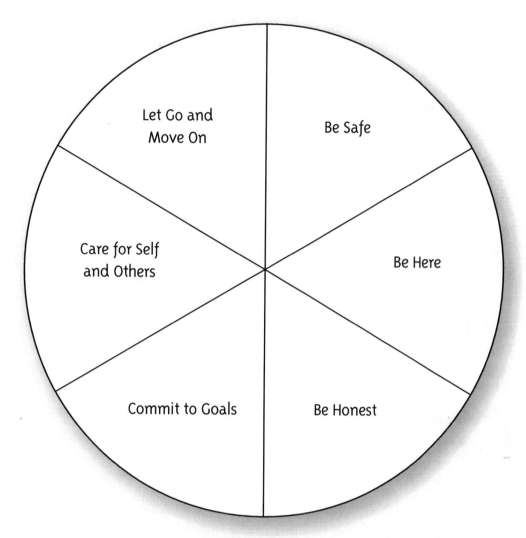

2. When you are finished, find a partner and share your ideas for each Full Value.

New Ideas: (write any new ideas that you discussed here)

Where RU?

Control to Empowerment—Assessment of Your Group

Write in your group members' names on the level you think they have achieved this _____ (teacher to fill in desired time period).

Level 10

Level 9

Level 8

Level 7

Level 6

Level 5

Level 4

Level 3

Level 2

Level 1

TOTAL TEAM SCORE: _____

AVERAGE SCORE: _____

DATE: _____

Learning Log

Name: _____

Write your thoughts on one of the following questions:

- ❏ What I learned was…
- ❏ What surprised me was…
- ❏ Right now, I'm feeling…
- ❏ I want to know…

_____

_____

_____

Circle the number that represents your team's ranking. (5= excellent; 1= poor)

Your team's creative thinking	1	2	3	4	5
Your team's problem solving	1	2	3	4	5
Your team's decision making	1	2	3	4	5

Topic:	
LOOKS LIKE	**SOUNDS LIKE**

Topic:	
LOOKS LIKE	**SOUNDS LIKE**

Name: _____

QUALITY CONTROL

CIRCLE the description that fits you!

	ONE	**TWO**	**THREE**	**FOUR**
Full Value Contract	does not behave inline with the group's Full Values	occasionally behaves inline with the group's Full Values	most of the time behaves consistent with the group's Full Values	always behaves consistently with the group's Full Values
Work Together	no effort made to establish positive group relationships	sometimes makes effort to establish group relationships	establishes positive relationship with group members most of the time	establishes positive relationship with group members all of the time
Safe Environment (Physical)	no effort to create a safe physical space	some effort made to create and maintain a safe physical space	effort is made most of the time to create and maintain a safe physical space	effort is always made to create and maintain a safe physical space
Safe Environment (Emotional)	no effort to create a safe emotional space	some effort made to create and maintain a safe emotional space	effort is made most of the time to create and maintain a safe emotional space	effort is always made to create and maintain a safe emotional space
TOTAL SCORE:				

Group GRAB

For each of the following GRAB areas, reflect on your group and/or answer the questions and then rank your group on a scale from 1-10. (1-being worst and 10-being the best) by circling the number. Please give examples explaining your score.

Goals: Does the group support individual goals? Do members understand the goals of the group?

1   2   3   4   5   6   7   8   9   10

comments: _____

_____

_____

Readiness: Do group members participate on a regular basis? Can the group push through their frustration?

1   2   3   4   5   6   7   8   9   10

comments: _____

_____

_____

Affect: Is there an understanding of feelings? Can feelings be expressed without devaluing others?

1   2   3   4   5   6   7   8   9   10

comments: _____

_____

_____

Behavior: Does the group demonstrate responsible behavior? Do group members help one another?

1   2   3   4   5   6   7   8   9   10

comments: _____

_____

_____

Add up each of the scores _____   TOTAL: _____

Thinking Errors

THINKING ERROR	THOUGHT	PAYOFF/CONSEQUENCE
Victim Stance	"Other people got me into this situation. It's their fault."	You don't have to take responsibility for your actions/ You are always looking for people to fix things for you.
Lying by Omission	"I didn't lie to you. I just know more than I am saying."	You can lie to others about who you really are/ You cannot trust others since you assume they lie like you.
Closed Channel	"I'm perfect; the mistakes I make are not my fault."	You can keep doing what you want to do/ You keep making the same mistakes.
I Can't	"I can't" (inside you are saying, "I don't want to.")	You don't have to put any effort into tasks/ you do not grow and accomplish little.
Jumping to Conclusions	"I can tell from the way he looked at me that he wants to fight!"	You are always right/ You make poor decisions based on inaccurate information.
Grandiosity	"I am better than you; don't question me--you don't get it."	You get to do what you want/ You continually make the same mistakes.
Minimizing	"Stealing from them doesn't matter because they are rich."	Your actions become unimportant/ You never take responsibility for your actions.
Shoulds/Oughts	"I should act better; I shouldn't hate him so much."	You can rebel against yourself/You can't connect your actions with your wishes.
Vagueness	"I don't know; Maybe; I guess."	Unclear avoids being pinned/ no growth from lack of commitment
Lack of Empathy	"I'm the REAL victim here, If you would take care of me, I wouldn't have to hurt others"	You are entitled to be selfish/ You end up abusing many people.
Awfulizing	"This is terrible and unbearable."	You do not have to deal with anything unpleasant/ You never learn to solve problems or tolerate discomfort.
Lack of Time Perspective	"I have to have this RIGHT NOW!"	You do not have to delay gratification/ You do not learn resilience or self control.
Power/Control	"I am bigger and meaner than you'll ever be; I'm in control"	You get people to do what you want/ You do not know how to have balanced relationships.

Wearing Someone Else's Glasses

Name: _____ Date: _____

Find witnesses that can show evidence of you showing each full value

FULL VALUE ATTRIBUTE	EVIDENCE	WITNESS
BE HERE		
BE SAFE		
BE HONEST		
SET GOALS		
CARE FOR SELF AND OTHERS		
LET GO AND MOVE ON		

Individual Goal Setting Sheet

Name: _____ Date: _____

What do I want to accomplish during the next week at (what goal have I set)?

_____

_____

_____

_____

_____

How can I accomplish it (what actions am I willing to take)?

_____

_____

_____

_____

_____

What resources will help me? (my goal partner, other group members, other people)?

_____

_____

_____

_____

_____

How will I know if I am reaching my goal (how will I measure it – on Friday I will know I have achieved my goal because…)?

_____

_____

_____

_____

_____

Goal Partner Worksheet — To Complete with Your Partner

Name: _____ Date: _____

Name of Goal Partner: _____

My goal(s) is:

_____

_____

_____

How is it:

Specific? _____

_____

Measurable? _____

_____

Achievable? _____

_____

Relevant? _____

_____

Trackable? _____

_____

I agree to work on the above goal(s)   I agree to help with my partner's goal(s)

_____   _____
Signature   Partner's Signature

Feelings Spectrum

MAD	SAD	GLAD	AFRAID
Bothered	Down	At Ease	Uneasy
Ruffled	Blue	Secure	Apprehensive
Irritated	Somber	Comfortable	Careful
Displeased	Low	Relaxed	Cautious
Annoyed	Glum	Optimistic	Hesitant
Steamed	Lonely	Satisfied	Tense
Irked	Disappointed	Refreshed	Anxious
Perturbed	Worn Out	Stimulated	Nervous
Frustrated	Melancholy	Pleased	Edgy
Angry	Downhearted	Warm	Distressed
Fed Up	Unhappy	Snug	Scared
Disgusted	Dissatisfied	Happy	Frightened
Indignant	Gloomy	Encouraged	Repulsed
Ticked Off	Mournful	Tickled	Agitated
Fuming	Grieved	Proud	Afraid
Explosive	Depressed	Cheerful	Overwhelmed
Enraged	Lousy	Delighted	Frantic
Irate	Crushed	Thrilled	Panic Stricken
Incensed	Defeated	Joyful	Horrified
Burned Up	Dejected	Elated	Petrified
Outraged	Empty	Exhilarated	Terrified
Furious	Wretched	Overjoyed	Numb
	Despairing	Ecstatic	
	Devastated		

CONFUSED	ASHAMED	LONELY
Curious	Uncomfortable	Out of place
Uncertain	Awkward	Left-out
Ambivalent	Clumsy	Unheeded
Doubtful	Self-conscious	Lonesome
Unsettled	Disconcerted	Disconnected
Hesitant	Chagrinned	Remote
Perplexed	Abashed	Invisible
Puzzled	Embarrassed	Unwelcome
Muddled	Flustered	Cut-off
Distracted	Sorry	Excluded
Flustered	Apologetic	Insignificant
Jumbled	Ashamed	Ignored
Fragmented	Remorseful	Neglected
Dismayed	Guilty	Separated
Insecure	Disgusted	Removed
Bewildered	Belittled	Detached
Lost	Humiliated	Isolated
Stunned	Violated	Unwanted
Chaotic	Dirty	Rejected
Torn	Mortified	Deserted
Baffled	Defiled	Outcast
Dumbfounded	Devastated	Abandoned
	Degraded	Desolate
		Forsaken

References

Collard, Mark, *No Props*: Beverly, MA, Project Adventure, 2005.

Cooper, Robert K. and Ayman Sawaf, Executive EQ: *Emotional Intelligence in Leadership Organizations*: NY, Grosset/Putnam, 1997.

Goleman, Daniel, "Emotional Intelligence: Why It Can Matter More than IQ", Learning Journal, May-June, 1996.

Goleman, Daniel, *Working with Emotional Intelligence*: NY, Bantam Dell, 1998.

Panicucci, Jane et al, *Adventure Curriculum for Physical Education*: Middle School: Beverly, MA, Project Adventure, 2002.

Rohnke, Karl and Steve Butler, *Quicksilver*: Dubuque, IA, Kendall Hunt Publishing, 1995.

Schoel, Jim, Dick Prouty and Paul Radcliffe, *Islands of Healing*: Hamilton, MA, Project Adventure 1988.

Schoel, Jim and Rich Maizell, *Exploring Islands of Healing*: Beverly, MA, Project Adventure, 2002

Weisinger, Hendrie, *Emotional Intelligence at Work*: San Francisco, CA, Jossey-Bass, 1998.